BUILDING THE KINGDOM

A HISTORY OF THE CATHOLIC CHURCH

BY ROBBIE PEÑATE

LIFE TEEN

Unless otherwise noted, Scripture passages have been taken from the Revised Standard Version, Catholic edition. Copyright ©1946, 1952, 1971 by the Division of Christian Education of the National Council of the Churches of Christ in the USA. Used by permission. All rights reserved.

Quotes are taken from the English translation of the Catechism of the Catholic Church for the United States of America (indicated as CCC), 2nd ed. Copyright ©1997 by United States Catholic Conference – Libreria Editrice Vaticana.

©2015 Life Teen, Inc. All rights reserved. No part of this book, including interior design, cover design, and/or icons, may be reproduced or transmitted in any form, by any means (electronic, photocopying, recording, or otherwise) without prior written permission from the publisher.

The views and opinions expressed within this work are those of the author and do not necessarily reflect the views of Life Teen.

The information contained herein is published and produced by Life Teen, Inc. The resources and practices are in full accordance with the Roman Catholic Church. The Life Teen® name and associated logos are trademarks registered with the United States Patent and Trademark Office. Use of the Life Teen® trademarks without prior permission is forbidden. Permission may be requested by contacting Life Teen, Inc. at 480-820-7001.

Authored by Robbie Peñate.

Designed by Casey Olson.

Copy editing by Rachel Peñate and Joel Stepanek.

ISBN: 978-0-9962385-3-3

Published by Life Teen, Inc.
2222 S. Dobson Rd.
Suite 601
Mesa, AZ 85202

LifeTeen.com
Printed in the United States of America.
Printed on acid-free paper.

For more information about Life Teen or to order additional copies, go online to LifeTeen.com or call us at 1-800-809-3902.

TABLE OF CONTENTS

INTRODUCTION
pg v

CHAPTER 1
A Faith Set On Fire - From Pentecost to Nero
pg 1

CHAPTER 2
The Five Good Emperors - The Edict of Milan
pg 7

CHAPTER 3
You Can't Love What You Don't Know - The Christological Heresies
pg 15

CHAPTER 4
Timber! - The Fall of Rome
pg 23

CHAPTER 5
Change is Hard - The Rise of Christendom
pg 29

CHAPTER 6
A New Religion Rises - The Rise of Islam
pg 35

CHAPTER 7
Like a Really Bad Breakup - The Great Schism
pg 39

CHAPTER 8
Jerusalem, Our Home - The Crusades
pg 45

CHAPTER 9
Popes vs. Kings - The Avignon Papacy
pg 53

CHAPTER 10
The Crusades' Misunderstood Sister - The Inquisition
pg 61

CHAPTER 11
Catholic *is* Christian - The Protestant Reformation
pg 67

CHAPTER 12
The Gift of Faith *and* Reason - The Enlightenment
pg 73

CHAPTER 13
A Divine Software Update - Vatican II
pg 79

CHAPTER 14
New Heralds of Faith - St. John Paul II and the Modern Church
pg 85

EPILOGUE
The Universal Call to Sainthood - The Future Is Yours
pg 91

- INTRODUCTION -

Jesus began His public ministry with the phrase, "the kingdom of God is at hand; repent and believe in the gospel" (Mark 1:15). From that moment on, God's Kingdom in heaven was being built on earth in the form of the Catholic Church. The story begins with Jesus, but it doesn't end there. After Jesus' death on the cross, His Apostles continued the work of preaching the Gospel to the ends of the earth. They continued to build the Kingdom that had been founded by Jesus on St. Peter (Matthew 16:18). As the Apostles began to die, the work of building God's Kingdom became the work of a new generation of Christians. For 2,000 years, the responsibility of building God's Kingdom has been handed down from believer to believer, each doing their part to honor God with their lives. Today, this responsibility falls to us. God has given the Church to us as a gift, handed down from Jesus Himself, and it is our turn to continue to build it up and invite others to do the same. But *we cannot fully appreciate this wonderful gift we have been given if we do not know the history of it.* It's like any other gift: when you understand the sacrifices that someone has gone through to give it to you, it means a whole lot more.

So let's not think about the history of the Church as just a bunch of names and dates and facts; that's too much like school—I should know, I'm a teacher. The history of the Church is so much more than that! It is the dramatic story of how God desires to bring salvation to the whole world through His Son, Jesus Christ. It's the tale of our older brothers and sisters in Christ and everything they endured for their faith and their love of God. It's the evidence that God is still at work in the world and that He has not simply abandoned us to our own devices. It's the work of the Holy Spirit leading all men, women, and children back to the Father. And it's a preview of what you and I can accomplish when we remain faithful to the King of Kings and Lord of Lords. Those who have gone before us in Christ have handed on to us a great tradition of faith and we would be remiss if we didn't learn to appreciate it.

In this book, you will read about many great members of the Church and the incredible lengths they went to build up God's Kingdom here on earth. *But despite everything that they did already, there is still so much work to do and each and every one of must play a part.* The Kingdom won't be complete unless you and I do our job, and we can't do that job well unless we know what others already did and how it happened. That would be like inheriting a half-finished house and trying to finish building it without looking and seeing what the previous workers already constructed! I hope that by the time you finish this book you have a greater knowledge of our shared past, and a desire to be a greater part of Building the Kingdom in the future.

1

A FAITH SET ON FIRE
– FROM PENTECOST TO NERO –

The Catholic Church was born from the side of Jesus Christ as He hung upon the Cross.

Maybe that sounds weird, but it's exactly what happened. I'm not saying that a physical building came out of Jesus' side along with blood and water, but this was the defining moment for the Catholic Church. It was at this moment that God paid the ransom for the world and opened the door to salvation. It was at this moment that the gates of Heaven were opened and all of humanity was redeemed by Jesus Christ.

Looking back, in light of the Resurrection, we can see the good that God brought out of the evil of the Crucifixion. But in the moment, I can't imagine the fear that came over the Apostles, or anyone who had followed Jesus. Indeed, we do know that the Apostles were scared. Not only did they run away when Jesus was arrested, but after His death they locked themselves in a room. They were afraid that they might be next (John 20:19). One can only imagine that the Apostles were an ancient inspiration for Hollywood's *The Purge*.

If the Apostles had remained in their fear, the Church as we know it today would not exist, the Gospel of Jesus Christ would not have been spread, and it would be much harder to know Jesus Christ and His love for us. Luckily, God knew that the Apostles were afraid. He knew that they needed a little pep talk to go out and "make disciples of all nations" as He had commanded (Matthew 28:19). So, God sent them the Holy Spirit to give them the grace to do what He had called them to do.

Isn't this still strikingly true for us today – our fear of the unknown? God calls us to do great things. But first, He calls us to step out of our comfort zones, out of our "locked rooms." Throughout my life, I've realized my own "locked room" is that reoccurring fear of inadequacy – I'm not good enough, smart enough, or cool enough to make an impact in people's lives. There have been many times that this fear has prevented me from reaching out to someone in need or starting something new. But the times when I have taken that leap of faith and stepped out of my "locked room," I have seen God do amazing things through me. Maybe you are like me, suffering from feelings of inadequacy. Or maybe your locked room is depression, anxiety, or fear of the unknown. Whatever your locked room is, God wants to help you unlock that door. He wants to give you the grace of the Holy Spirit so that you can do incredible things. It won't always be easy, but remember that He will give us the grace to be successful in accomplishing His work. But I digress, back to the story…

The Apostles received the grace of the Holy Spirit on the Feast of Pentecost. Many people call Pentecost the "birthday of the Church." But I think that is a bad name for it. Like I said earlier, the Church is born from the side of Jesus as He hung upon the Cross. The descent of the Holy Spirit at Pentecost is really more like the Baptism of the Church. The Church existed before the descent of the Holy Spirit, but when Mary and the Apostles receive the Holy Spirit, it is then that they begin to do the work of the Lord. We existed before our Baptism, but when we are baptized we receive the Holy Spirit and the grace to do the Lord's work. Here is how that event is recorded in the Book of the Acts of the Apostles:

> When the day of Pentecost had come, they were all together in one place. And suddenly a sound came from heaven like the rush of a mighty wind, and it filled all the house where they were sitting. And there appeared to them tongues as of fire, distributed and resting on each of them. And they were all filled with the Holy Spirit and began to speak in other tongues, as the Spirit gave them utterance. (Acts 2:1-4)

The Apostles, upon receiving the Holy Spirit, began to preach the Gospel of Jesus to some of the people who just had Him put to death. Talk about intimidating! But, indeed the Apostles continued to preach with great courage. And through the power of the Holy Spirit, they were able to spread the Gospel *in different languages* to Jews from all over the world. Think about it. That is incredible! And it serves to tell us that the Gospel is universal, meant for all people. In fact, this is what the word "Catholic" means. It is from this place, this room in Jerusalem, through the courage of the Apostles and the grace of the Holy Spirit, that the Catholic Church would be spread to the entire world. Just a handful of people, with little or no education, wealth, or possessions, essentially built the Church as we know it today. *Never doubt how much you can change the world if you just follow God's plan!*

Unfortunately, though, for the Apostles, this new-found courage did not give them a new-found invincibility. As a matter of fact, the only Apostle to die a natural death was St. John. He died in exile – a fate far less gruesome than that of the other Apostles. Although the history of their deaths can be difficult to navigate, the tradition of the Church tells us that the Apostles died in the following ways:

- Peter was crucified upside down because he felt unworthy to die in the same manner as Jesus.

- James the Greater (older) was beheaded.

- Andrew was crucified on an x-shaped cross. Tradition tells us that he used every single last breath to preach the Gospel from his cross.

- Thomas was stabbed with a spear.

- James the Lesser (younger) was thrown off of the roof of the temple (about 100 feet), stoned, and beaten with clubs.

- Matthew was stabbed to death with swords.

- Bartholomew was skinned alive.

- Jude was shot full of arrows.

- Philip was crucified.

- Simon was axed to death.

- John was boiled alive, survived miraculously, and was then exiled to the island of Patmos.

- Judas Iscariot, Jesus' betrayer, hung himself, as is recorded in Sacred Scripture.

What an incredible lesson we have to learn from the Apostles: What are we willing to endure for our faith? We may not face the same bloody fate, but we too will have our faith challenged, and will face persecution for what we believe… we will face mockery, doubt, and perhaps even hatred. And, at some point we all have to answer this question: How much am I willing to put up with for Jesus' sake? What will our answer be?

As for the early Christians, the persecution and murder of the Apostles would not be the only violence they faced. Even during their own lifetime, others who began to follow the teachings of Jesus Christ were persecuted. Saul, who became St. Paul, arrested, imprisoned, and consented to the deaths of those who began to believe in Jesus as the Messiah (Acts 9). Those whom the Apostles converted in far away lands often faced persecution from their own culture as well. Despite heavy persecution from virtually every culture, Christianity quickly spread throughout the known world. Although it is not recorded in the book of the Acts of the Apostles, we know that Saint Peter and Saint Paul took the saving message of Jesus to Rome. It would be in Rome that the persecution of Christians would take on a new and more horrific form.

It is important to recall here how influential Rome was at this time. Rome itself was not just a city, but an empire. And not just any empire, but one of the greatest empires the world has ever seen. The Roman Empire would be the dominant empire in the world until at least the third century and as Christianity infiltrated the empire it began to spread wherever the empire did, but more on that in later chapters.

In the year 64 AD, there was a great fire in Rome that damaged or severely destroyed about one-third of the city. When the fire was finally brought under control six days later, the Roman people demanded that the perpetrators be brought to justice. Many people thought Nero was to blame, but in all likelihood he was not at fault. Nero, though, needed a scapegoat to take the heat off of him, (Get it? Heat, because there was a fire.) and so he quickly pointed fingers at the Christians.

Christians were easy targets. They worshipped one God instead of many (which was very odd for ancient Rome) and therefore were constantly blamed for the bad things that happened throughout the Empire. If there was a drought, it was the Christians' fault because they didn't worship the god of the rain. So, when Rome was ravaged by the fire Nero blamed the Christians, and as punishment made it illegal for them to practice their Christian faith. When Christians were caught, Nero had numerous ways to make them suffer.

The punishments that Nero inflicted upon the Christians of the city of Rome were so severe that many historians today suggest that he suffered from mental illness. This notion is supported by the fact that his uncle, Caligula, acted erratically and also appeared to be mentally unstable. (I mean the guy once went so far as to try and name his horse as the consul of Rome, which was the highest elected official at the time.) Nero, however, turned killing Christians into a sport, and during his reign many Christians were brutally killed for refusing to renounce their faith. Nero would take Christians, dip them in tar, and then light them on fire so that his garden was illuminated as he walked through it at night. If that wasn't bad enough, he was also known to sew animal skins onto Christians who were chained down, and release his starving hunting dogs who would eat them alive.

The most famous martyr during the reign of Nero is Saint Peter. Peter, the first pope, was living in Rome at the time of the Great Fire. Church tradition tells us that when Nero blamed Christians and began arresting and torturing them. As the leader of the Christian Church, Peter was a high-value target. Like Katniss Everdeen in *Mockingjay*, Peter was seen as the face of the "revolutionaries." So, Peter snuck out of the city encouraged by others to seek protection. But, as he was leaving, something convinced him to go back. On the road outside of Rome, Peter had a vision of Jesus walking toward the city. As Peter approached, he asked, "*Quo vadis domine?*" which means, "Where are you going Lord?" And Jesus responds, "*Romam vado iterum crufigi.*" "I am going to Rome to be crucified again." Peter was at once cut to the heart. And the guilt weighed heavily upon him as he recognized the threat of death he was running away from was a threat Jesus so willingly accepted. So, Peter turned around, and with his head held high, walked back into Rome. Within a matter of months, Peter was arrested and sentenced to death. He was crucified upside down in Nero's Circus, which stood in the place where St. Peter's Basilica stands today. **Nero attempted to destroy Peter's legacy, but in the end it is Peter's legacy that is built over Nero's.**

Nero limited his persecution of Christians to the city of Rome itself. He did not make it legal for Christians to be killed throughout the Empire. But Nero would not be the only emperor to use the Christians as scapegoats. Successive emperors would make it legal to kill Christians in every corner of the Empire and would create new and more horrible tortures to try and make the Christians renounce their belief in the Risen Christ. For 250 years after the Fire of Rome, Christians would be persecuted throughout the Roman Empire at the hands of the emperors. Think about how long that is. 250 years ago, the United States of America didn't even exist yet. And yet, despite the profound dangers that came with conversion to Christianity, it was during this period of time that we saw some of the greatest growth in the Church. As the second century theologian Tertullian once wrote, "The blood of martyrs is the seed of the Church."

REFLECTION QUESTIONS:

1. What is one thing you are afraid will happen if you live your faith in a radical way?

2. How much suffering would you be willing to endure for your faith? Why?

3. How is it that we suffer for our faith in today's world? What can we learn from St. Peter's example?

2

THE FIVE GOOD EMPERORS
- THE EDICT OF MILAN -

For almost 300 years after the death of Jesus Christ, Christians throughout the Roman Empire were heavily persecuted. Some of the heaviest of these persecutions came during the reign of the "Five Good Emperors:" Nerva, Trajan, Hadrian, Antonius-Pius, and Marcus Aurelius. These men were known as "good" because they improved the Empire economically and architecturally, not because of their morality. To give you an idea of how bad things were, let's take a look at the man who was probably the nicest to Christians.

Emperor Trajan developed a policy for persecuting Christians that was considered "moderate." Early in the second century, Emperor Trajan was asked how he should deal with the Christians. Trajan's response was harsh and unforgiving. Essentially he said, "Don't go looking for them, but if one is brought to you and you can prove they are a Christian, they deserve to die." Moderate? Hah! Funny joke... Think about that for a minute. The best-case scenario for Christians was that the government wasn't going to hunt them down, but if their neighbors turned them in, it was all over.

Can you imagine the extreme terror that the Christians of the time must have felt? Many Christians lived their entire lives knowing nothing but this fear. They faced death even though they were doing nothing wrong. They lived in constant fear that soldiers would knock at their door and arrest them. Everyone they met could have turned them in for being a Christian. And yet, their faith must have been so much stronger than their fear because they continued to follow Jesus! They continued to worship Him on Sunday, to live their lives in a radically different way than the rest of their community.

Imagine if we had that kind of faith today. Imagine if we weren't afraid that others would find out we are Catholic. Imagine if we lived lives that were radically different than the lives of the people around us. Imagine if we lived lives that were focused on others instead of ourselves; if we lived lives of forgiveness instead of holding grudges; if we only took what we needed and used the rest to help others. How different would our world be?

This is the way in which the early Church lived. They combated the fear and persecution they faced with radical love. Not only did they love Jesus Christ and the Church, they loved even their enemies, just as Jesus had commanded. It was this radical love that attracted people to Christianity, despite the dangers involved with becoming a Christian. People saw the love that the Christians had for one another, and even for complete strangers! They saw how joyful the Christians were, even in the face of torture and death. The following is part of a letter written during the second century, called the "Epistle (or letter) to Diognetus" that explains why people were so amazed by Christians:

> Christians are indistinguishable from other men either by nationality, language or customs. They do not inhabit separate cities of their own, or speak a strange dialect, or follow some outlandish way of life....
>
> **And yet there is something extraordinary about their lives.** They live in their own countries as though they were only passing through.... Any country can be their homeland, but for them their homeland, wherever it may be, is a foreign country.... they share their meals, but not their wives. They live in the flesh, but they are not governed by the desires of the flesh. They pass their days upon earth, but they are citizens of heaven. Obedient to the laws, they yet live on a level that transcends the law.
>
> Christians love all men, but all men persecute them. Condemned because they are not understood, they are put to death, but raised to life again. They live in poverty, but enrich many.... They suffer dishonor, but that is their glory.... A blessing is their answer to abuse, deference their response to insult.... They are attacked by the Jews as aliens, they are persecuted by

the Greeks, yet no one can explain the reason for this hatred. (emphasis mine)

Many people credit St. Augustine with the saying, "The truth is like a lion. You don't have to defend it. Let it loose. It will defend itself." This is what the early Christians did; they lived their lives according to the teachings of Jesus Christ, who called Himself the Truth. Through the genuine witness of the early Christians, others were convinced of the truth of the Gospel message.

So we are faced with a difficult question: *Am I living a life according to the truth?* Could this "Epistle to Diognetus" be about me? Can someone look at my life and say, "There goes a disciple of Jesus Christ"? Being a Christian isn't just about going to Mass on Sunday and praying before we eat. Being a Christian is not just something we do, *it is who we are*! It means that we belong to Jesus Christ and that, in all things, we are trying to be like Him. We must allow the Holy Spirit to penetrate every aspect of our life so that we may be disciples of Jesus Christ in every way. We must conform our lives to Jesus so much that, with St. Paul, we may say, "I have been crucified with Christ; it is no longer I who live, but Christ who lives in me" (Galatians 2:20). Rest assured that becoming this kind of person, a saint, is not easy. We all struggle to do this and for almost all of us it will be a struggle to live our lives perfectly in conformity to the Gospel. But the more we try, the closer we will get to our goal. Let us identify those parts of our lives that do not reflect Jesus, and let us change, so that when others see us, they may only see Jesus Christ. As my friend Tyler used to say, let us "always present Jesus Christ as irresistible to the yearning human heart." May our lives always reveal the beauty of the Gospel, and through that authenticity may it attract others to Christ.

Early Christians managed to change the world by the way they lived their lives. They endured their hardships with love, hope, and faith and brought many others to Jesus. They believed that their hardships would not last forever and the severe persecutions officially came to an end in the year 313 AD thanks to the Roman Emperor Constantine. Only one year earlier, in 312 AD, while preparing for a battle, Constantine had a vision in which he saw a chi-rho (Px) in the sky and heard the words, "In this sign, you shall conquer." He quickly had his soldiers paint the symbol on their shields before going into battle. He returned later to Rome victorious in battle and eager to thank the God who had helped him in combat. He learned that the symbol he had seen was a Christian symbol. Constantine soon converted to Christianity and in the year

313 AD he issued the **Edict of Milan**, making it legal for Christians to practice their faith openly.

Many Christians lost their lives during the persecutions led by the Roman Empire, and a few of those lives stand out in a special way:

ST. IGNATIUS OF ANTIOCH

Arrested in the year 107 AD in Antioch by Emperor Trajan, St. Ignatius was taken back to Rome to be executed. On his way to Rome he wrote seven letters to different churches along the way. In his final letter, he urged the Church in Rome to not try and stop his martyrdom. He wrote to them saying, "The only thing I ask of you is to allow me to offer the libation of my blood to God. I am the wheat of the Lord; may I be ground by the teeth of the beasts to become the immaculate bread of Christ."[1] Just a few days later he was killed by lions. Although many people remember his bravery, few people remember that St. Ignatius was the first to use the term "Catholic Church,"[2] in his letter to the Christians at Smyrna. He also told people that they should listen to their bishops, because the bishop represented Jesus Christ and the Catholic Church was centered on Jesus.

ST. POLYCARP OF SMYRNA

St. Polycarp was Bishop of the city of Smyrna and a good friend of St. Ignatius of Antioch. Polycarp was arrested for being a Christian and sentenced to be burned to death. When they lit the fire around him people reported that the fire smelled like incense instead of burning flesh. Only a few moments later, people noticed that Polycarp was not burning! He was standing in the middle of the fire completely unharmed! Since he would not burn, soldiers stabbed him to death. The eyewitness account of Polycarp's martyrdom was recorded and is known as *The Martyrdom of Polycarp* because we are very clever at naming things.

ST. JUSTIN MARTYR

St. Justin was a convert to Christianity late in his life. He had been a philosopher and became one of the Church's earliest apologists. (An apologist is one who defends the teachings of the Church.) In one of his writings from the early second century, St. Justin described the Mass in the following way:

On the day we call the day of the sun, all who dwell in the city or country gather in the same place. The memoirs of the apostles and the writings of the prophets are read [and] he who presides over those gathered admonishes and challenges them to imitate these beautiful things. Then we all rise together and offer prayers for ourselves... and for all others, wherever they may be... When the prayers are concluded we exchange the kiss [of peace]. Then someone brings bread and a cup of water and wine mixed together to him who presides over the brethren. He takes them and... he gives thanks (in Greek: eucharistian) that we have been judged worthy of these gifts. When he has concluded the prayers and thanksgivings, all present give voice to an acclamation by saying: "Amen." When he who presides has given thanks and the people have responded, those whom we call deacons give to those present the "eucharisted" bread, wine and water and take them to those who are absent.

Although the Edict of Milan ended legal persecution of Christians, the persecution continued at the hands of many Roman citizens. These persecutions of Christians are similar to the way people persecute others today based on the color of their skin. Although segregation has been outlawed in the United States, there are still many people who choose not to treat people of other races with dignity and equality. There were many people who still hated Christians and mistreated them and even killed them. In fact, in many parts of the world today, especially in the Middle East, Christians are persecuted for their faith. There are still people who are being martyred for following Jesus Christ. This is not a reality for most of us who live in the United States and so we often take it for granted. But for many Christians, the possibility of martyrdom is a fear they live with everyday.

I have to admit, when I first started learning the stories of the martyrs I was horrified. Each time I heard a story about someone who refused to renounce the name of Jesus I was screaming in my head, "Just pretend! Tell them what they want to hear so that you can save your life! I'm sure God will understand and forgive you if you just lie to them and tell them you don't believe in Him!" At the time I was still very new to my faith and I gladly would have lied about loving Jesus if it meant someone would stop torturing me. And so I kept asking myself, why would these men and women keep telling their torturers, "I am a Christian"?

The reason they wouldn't lie was because being a Christian wasn't just something they did or believed, it was who they were. They had fallen so deeply in love with Jesus Christ and His Church that their very identity was as a Christian. Today, we very rarely identify ourselves in just one way. As a matter of fact, we tend to shy away from "labels" because we are afraid that if we commit to something we will miss out on something better. But if we do state our identity, it is often in ways that only describe a part of us. For instance when I was very young I used to define myself as a good student. My whole identity was based on my grades and on being a well behaved. I guess what I am trying to say is that I was definitely a "teacher's pet." In fact, I was so caught up with getting good grades and being a good student that when I was in elementary school I remember, on multiple occasions, crying because the teacher got mad at me. Eventually I grew out of defining myself by my grades and started defining myself as an athlete. Sports, especially baseball, became everything to me. I remember being so caught up in being a good baseball player that the water works would start if I struck out or lost a game. And then when I didn't make my high school baseball team I was devastated, but at least by then I had learned not to cry. At least not in public.

The point isn't that I used to be a cry baby, or that my dreams of becoming a professional baseball player haven't come true (yet), but rather that during those moments of my life, I could not imagine ever saying to someone, "I want to fail this class," or "I hate baseball," regardless of what was going on in my life. To do so would have been to deny who I was. This is why the martyrs can't deny Jesus. If they did, they would lose all sense of who they were. It would be as if they were saying they didn't even exist. These brave men and women who gave up their lives for love of God deserve our respect and reverence. We should look to them as examples of how much we can and should love Jesus and His Church.

Despite the fact that few of us will face a red martyrdom, that is, a physical death for our faith, we are called to a white martyrdom. White martyrdom means that although we may never shed our blood, we are called to die to ourselves so that we may live for Christ. Too often, the things we desire are not the things we should, so the Church calls us to die to those desires so that we can truly live for Jesus. This might mean giving up our desire for popularity by choosing not to see a certain movie, or listen to certain music. Or maybe it means letting others ridicule us because we choose to befriend the unpopular people at our school and avoid parties where we know we might be in the near occasion of sin. Remember that Jesus told us that the world would hate us if we follow Him (Matthew 10:22). I don't mean that we should go out and purposefully make enemies, but we should never compromise our faith or our values for others. Essentially, white martyrdom consists of desiring sainthood above all else; above popularity, money, power, fame, everything. *When we can truly die to these other desires, we will live more perfectly for Jesus and find the thing that will make us most happy.*

Let us pray now for our brothers and sisters in Christ who are in danger of death:

Heavenly Father, I pray today for all of those Christians around the world who practice their faith in fear. I ask that you would grant them the courage to continue to love and follow you no matter what. I ask that you would grant them the protection of the Holy Spirit; preserve their lives so that they may continue to love and serve you and your people. I pray also for all of those who have lost their lives rather than turn their backs on you. May they rest in the peace of your Son, Jesus Christ, and may we one day be lucky enough to join them in your loving presence. Amen.

REFLECTION QUESTIONS:

1. Christians were persecuted primarily because their beliefs were different than those of the people around them. How do you see people being persecuted today because of their beliefs?

2. The martyrs were able to endure great suffering because their whole identity was found in Jesus Christ. Where do you find your identity? How can you start finding your identity more in Jesus?

3. All Christians are called to white martyrdom. What are the things/desires in your life that lead you away from Jesus that you need to "die to" so that you can live more perfectly for Jesus?

3

YOU CAN'T LOVE WHAT YOU DON'T KNOW
– THE CHRISTOLOGICAL HERESIES –

Do you know who Manti Te'o is? He is a football player. In college he played at the University of Notre Dame, and he was drafted by the San Diego Chargers to play in the NFL. Even if you aren't a sports fan, you might still recognize his name. That's because a few years ago he was involved in a catfishing scheme (an online scam involving the creation of a fake identity). And by involved I mean caught totally unaware. In Te'o's case, he met a girl online named Lennay Kekua and over the course of time he fell in love with her. After they had been a couple for some time, he was devastated to learn that she had died from injuries in a tragic car accident. During a period of mourning, he learned that she had never existed in the first place, and that it had all been an elaborate scheme to mess with him. In fact, "she" turned out to be a "he" and Te'o certainly did not love him.

You can't *really* love someone if you don't know them. This was a problem that the early Church faced. People began to have misconceptions about who Jesus is, and began to love this new "Jesus" rather than the real one, and that was a problem.

After issuing the Edict of Milan that gave legal protection to Christians, Constantine began to really emphasize Christianity throughout the

Roman Empire. You could say that he became the Church's biggest fan. He went out of his way to make it easier for people to be Christian. For instance, he banned many professions from working on Sunday so that people could obey the commandment to keep the Lord's Day holy. He also provided money for Christians to build churches so that they could worship. Until these early churches were built, Christians celebrated the Mass in their homes because it was dangerous to worship God in public.

Because of Constantine's love for the Catholic Church, people of many different religions began converting to Catholicism. At first, it was great, and the Church experienced a growth similar to that which we read about at the end of Acts 2 (when large numbers of people became Christian at once). Unfortunately it wasn't all sunshine and rainbows. Many people became Christian out of a sincere love for Jesus and His Church, but there were many who became Christian for the wrong reasons. Some became Christian because they wanted more political power; if the emperor was now a Christian, they thought they should be too. Others became Christian because Constantine allowed Christians to pay less in taxes; if governments offered that today we might just convert most of the world. Because of the new popularity of Christianity, the Church was opened up to heresies – a religious teaching contrary to the truth about Jesus and His teachings.

These heresies spread quickly and, for a variety of reasons, they became popular belief:

1. **As more and more people became Christian, it was harder and harder to make sure that everyone believed the truth.** When a false teaching surfaced, it wasn't only a few people in one city who needed correction, but many people all across the known world. And the pope couldn't just call them up – each by name – and correct them.

2. **Those who became Christian for the wrong reasons (the "false converts") didn't really care if they were spreading false teachings.** They had no interest in loving and worshipping God in truth, they just wanted the benefits that Christians were receiving.

3. **False teachings are often easier to believe.** Jesus calls us to change our lives, and that is hard. Sometimes it is easier to change who Jesus is than it is to change ourselves.

As heresies grew and spread, the Church established what is called "the catechumenate" as a way to teach people who Jesus is and what it means to follow Him. Now maybe you're sitting there thinking that becoming a Christian shouldn't be so hard, you just love Jesus. And in one sense you are right. But remember that being a Christian isn't just something you do on Sunday, it is something that should affect every moment of every day. By going through the catechumenate process, someone learns what the Church teaches, why she teaches that, and if they want to be a part of that. Today, this is most similar to RCIA, the Rite of Christian Initiation for Adults.

Unfortunately, during the time of Constantine the Church was growing so fast that it was impossible to teach everyone everything that the Church believed, causing many people to develop false ideas of who Jesus was and what He wants for our lives. Maybe knowing who Jesus is seems a little unimportant, but that couldn't be farther from the truth! Think about it, if we don't know who Jesus is, then we can't truly love Him. And if we can't love Him then how can we expect to have a good relationship with Him?

When I was little, I hated apples. I thought they were gross and I never wanted to eat them. But when I moved to Wisconsin, people thought I was crazy for not liking apples. They finally convinced me try one, and I loved it! I couldn't believe I had missed out on delicious apples for so long. It was like my whole life had been a lie to that point. I had a wrong belief about apples, and that changed the way I lived. Imagine living your entire life believing that Jesus isn't really the Son of God. Do you think that would change the way you act? Would that change the way you live your life? Of course it would! *What we believe affects how we act.*

Think about Lotso, the bear from *Toy Story 3*. When I first watched that movie, I really liked him at the beginning. He seemed like a nice Grandpa, walking with a cane, going out of his way to care for the other toys. But as the movie went on, I learned that Lotso is this tyrannical overlord with world domination in mind. And when I learned that Lotso was the bad guy, I no longer liked him. So I liked him when I had one belief about him, but when the truth came out my opinion about him changed. The same thing can happen if we have a wrong belief about Jesus, and *this is why heresies are so dangerous; we can end up basing our lives on a lie rather than on the truth.*

Today, the Church has a very well-defined teaching on who Jesus is and what He did. This teaching is known as the *hypostatic union*. It's a big word that means that Jesus had a human nature and a divine nature that were perfectly united. That means that Jesus is both perfectly God and perfectly human. Although this is what the Church has always believed, it was not always expressed well. Before the Church really knew how to express her beliefs about Jesus, several people expressed their beliefs about Him in ways that were wrong. These false teachings about Jesus are called Christological heresies because they are false teachings about who Jesus is. **Christological heresies** were the first heresies to really develop because being a Christian meant following Jesus. So it makes sense that the first controversy would be about who Jesus is. As time passed, new heresies would develop about other topics, like salvation and the Sacraments, but we will just focus on the Christological ones first.

ARIANISM

This was the first major heresy that the newly-legal Christian Church had to combat. Arianism was named after its founder, Arius. (Yup that's right, you start a heresy and we name it after you so nobody ever forgets you.) Arius believed and taught Jesus was not God, but that he was just very, very similar to God. He believed that God created Jesus and that therefore Jesus could not be God.

This teaching was very popular. The early Christians loved Arianism the way that fourteen-year-old girls love One Direction. In fact, they loved this teaching about Jesus so much that they began to attack people who did not believe it. They would break into churches where the Mass was being celebrated and would physically beat up people who believed that Jesus was truly God. And then those who believed that Jesus was truly God would attack those who believed that Jesus was not God. There was rioting in the streets and constant tension in Rome. You may be asking yourself at this point, "Seriously? Riots? It's not even a big deal." But for these early Christians it was a huge deal. They loved their faith so much that they took it very personally when someone told them they believed something wrong about Jesus.

This tension and rioting led Emperor Constantine to call the **Council of Nicaea** in the year 325 AD in order for the Church to clarify what she taught about Jesus. Bishops from all over the known world came to discuss who Jesus was and what teachings had been handed on about Him by the Church for the last 300 years. Arius was present at the Council to propose his ideas about Jesus. St. Nicholas, the guy who we based Santa Claus on, was also present. Why do I mention that? Because when he heard Arius teaching that Jesus was not God he got so angry that someone would say something so terrible about Him that he walked right up to Arius and punched him in the face. That's right everyone, Santa Claus hates heresy... and he spent three days in jail to prove it. Now I'm not advocating violence as a way to get Jesus' message across, but it sure sounds like it was worth it. When the Council of Nicaea was finally over, the Church declared that Jesus is made of the same substance as the Father, which is why today in the Nicene Creed we profess that Jesus is "consubstantial with the Father." Unfortunately, although the Council of Nicaea declared Arianism false, many continued to believe it and spread it.

APOLLINARIANISM

With Arianism still running rampant, many bishops looked for ways to prove it false. One such bishop was named Apollinaris. Apollinaris developed the idea that Jesus only had a human body, but that His soul was divine. He felt that this was a good response to the Arian heresy because it would prove that Jesus really was God if He had no human soul and only a human body. Well, it would have been a great answer to the problem of Arianism if it had not been such a terrible fit to the reality of Christ. The problem was that the Church had always taught that Jesus was **both** divine and human. Without a human mind and soul, Jesus could not have been truly human. The teachings of Apollinaris were declared to be heretical at the Council of Constantinople in the year 381 AD and the idea that Jesus did not have a human mind or soul became known as, you guessed it, Apollinarianism. Or maybe you didn't guess that because it is kind of a ridiculous word.

Both Arianism and Apollinarianism dealt directly with the very core of who Jesus was. As philosophers would say, that attacked the very nature of Jesus. And yet both heresies were wildly popular! People really wanted to know who Jesus was, and since the Church hadn't officially explained that Jesus was both fully God and fully man, these explanations seemed fairly reasonable to many.

NESTORIANISM

The next major heresy, developed by a bishop named Nestorious, was the heresy known as Nestorianism. He wanted to stop calling Mary the "theotokos" (a title meaning Mother of God) because he didn't really like the thought of a human being giving birth to God. Instead he wanted to call her the "Christotokos," to imply that Mary only gave birth to the human nature of Jesus. The major flaw with his argument is that never in the history of the world has a woman only given birth to a nature; women always give birth to a person.

And as a person, Jesus had two natures. St. Cyril of Alexandria set the record straight fairly quickly with a very simple argument. In fact the argument is so simple that even the most unskilled logicians (like myself) can understand it. Are you ready for it? Here it is: "Mary is the Mother of Jesus, and Jesus is God, so Mary is the Mother of God." I guess that is what passed for genius-level thinking back then. Nestorianism was ultimately condemned at the Council of Ephesus in 481 AD.

There were many other heresies regarding Jesus and many other councils setting them straight, but these three were probably the most popular and influential. In fact, Arianism was once so popular that it was said that, "The whole world had gone Arian." Despite the popularity of these different heresies, the fact that the truth of Jesus' nature was preserved is evidence that the Holy Spirit truly is guiding the Church. This is what Jesus promised the Apostles in the Gospel of John. He said to them, "When the Spirit of truth comes, He will guide you into all the truth..." (John 16:13). We trust that Jesus is true to His word and will not allow the Church to deviate from the truth.

The thing I find the most crazy about these three heresies is that the three men did not wake up one day and decide, "I want to be a heretic today." In fact, quite the opposite is true. These three men were very devout Christian priests. Unfortunately they seem to have had a prideful streak. They developed these ideas and theories about Jesus and when the Church declared these ideas to be wrong, they could not admit that they were wrong. They forgot that Jesus Christ promised to guide the Church into all truth. The same thing can happen to us today. When we encounter a teaching of the Church that we don't like or that we think is wrong, sometimes we forget that it is the Holy Spirit leading the Church toward the truth and we allow our pride to tell us that we are right and the Church is wrong. *Remember that one of the reasons that heresies can spread so quickly is because it is easier to change Jesus than it is to change ourselves.*

Whenever we find ourselves in this situation of disagreeing with the Church, we have to ask ourselves why we disagree. Too often we want Jesus to conform to our beliefs instead of trying to conform our lives to His teachings. Let us remember that Jesus is the same yesterday, today, and tomorrow. He does not change, but He does give us the grace to be more like Him, and it is only in becoming more like Him that we will find our true happiness.

REFLECTION QUESTIONS:

1. The more we know God the better we can love Him. How well do you know God the Father? Jesus? The Holy Spirit? What can you do to get to know them better?

2. When was the last time that your pride/ego caused you to do something you later regretted?

3. Our pride can be combatted by actively exercising humility, like when we give others honest compliments or do works of service. How can you be more humble in your every day actions?

4

TIMBER!
– THE FALL OF ROME –

One of my favorite games growing up was *Jenga*. It is an incredibly simple and thoroughly entertaining game. The best part of the game is pulling out that one block that makes the tower so unstable your opponent can't help but knock it down, or maybe I am just a little obsessed with winning.

The Roman Empire was like a giant *Jenga* tower. When it was first built it was strong and sturdy, but as time went on and key pieces were removed, the tower became more and more unstable, slowly becoming doomed to fall. But unlike the game Jenga, and very much like Humpty Dumpty, the pieces could not be put back together again.

Things really began to fall apart when the Empire split into two halves, the East and West. Today, the western half is commonly called the Roman Empire while the eastern half is referred to as the Byzantine Empire. This distinction is something that modern historians make because they can look back at how the split occurred, but at the time, people living in both halves of the Empire considered themselves Romans.

After Constantine moved the capitol of the Roman Empire from Rome to Constantinople in the year 330 AD, the western half of the Empire began to decline quickly. In just a few short years, Barbarian tribes from all around the Empire recognized the weakness of Rome and began to invade her borders. It was a free-for-all, a WWE smack down, a rage in the cage. By the year 410 AD, Barbarians invaded and sacked Rome, and in 476 AD, the last of the emperors of the western half of the Empire was overthrown. In retrospect, it probably wasn't that hard to overthrow him since he was a 14 year old boy.

Rome had fallen, and the empire that had survived for so many years was now gone. And I mean gone. There was nothing left of the grandeur of the west. The different invading tribes broke up the west into their own personal kingdoms, each wanting to conquer the land belonging to other tribes. If you have siblings, then you know exactly what it feels like to see something you want and not be able to just take it. Even the culture of these tribes was radically different from Rome. We call them "Barbarian" for a reason.

The Roman Empire was, in some sense of the word, "civilized." But, no one in their right mind would ever call these tribes civilized. Take, for example, a common form of "justice" in the tribes. To determine a person's guilt or innocence, the accused would be forced to grab a stone from the bottom of a boiling pot of water. Guilt would be determined by how long it took for the burns to heal, and disagreements would be settled by a fight to the death. Again, if you have siblings this might seem appealing, but it is certainly no way to run a civilization. But that's just the point. The tribes weren't interested in civilization. They had no interest in education, no desire to settle down and build communities that would last; their only desire was to go to war. And boy, were they good at it. They could kill and steal as well as anyone in history.

This decline in civilization in the west also led to a decline in fidelity to the Church. The Barbarian tribes had almost no interest in learning a faith contrary to their own pagan ones, and as they spread their culture, there was a general lowering of moral standards. It was very difficult for Catholics to remain faithful when everything around them was falling apart, and when the people who surrounded them were not faithful to Jesus Christ. There is a lesson to be learned here: *if we want to remain faithful to Jesus and to His Church, we need a strong community.* We need to surround ourselves with people who will help us to remain strong when it becomes difficult to live out our faith. The Catholics of this age knew this, and thus was born the monastic movement.

The monastic movement began before the fall of the West. The city of Rome was a difficult one to live in for Christians, even before Barbarians overran it. There were many pagan religions in Rome, and the moral standards weren't all that high, just read what St. Paul wrote about in his letter to the Romans:

> They were filled with all manner of wickedness, evil, covetousness, malice. Full of envy, murder, strife, deceit, malignity, they are gossips, slanderers, haters of God, insolent, haughty, boastful, inventors of evil, disobedient to parents, foolish, faithless, heartless, ruthless. (Romans 1:29-31)

That's pretty bad stuff, and with all of this going around, many Christians began to retreat from the city to live in community. And as Barbarians invaded and moral standards went down even more, increasing numbers of people chose to live monastic lives. But these monasteries weren't just important because they were places to live out their Christian lives freely, **they were also important because they helped to preserve Western Civilization as we know it.**

There are two major figures that we must talk about if we are going to talk about monasticism:

ST. ANTHONY OF THE DESERT

His is an incredible story. When he was roughly eighteen years old, his wealthy parents died suddenly, leaving him as their sole heir. Anthony heard the words of Jesus to the rich young man, "Go, sell what you have and give to the poor, and you will have treasure in heaven" (Mark 10:21). He sold his property to his neighbors, gave all the money to the poor, and moved into the desert to live his life in isolation as a hermit. With nothing to distract him, Anthony found plenty of time for prayer and reflection. Satan, seeing how Anthony's relationship with God grew, began to tempt him with boredom and laziness. There were even times when demons would appear and physically beat him to the point of unconsciousness. But all this did was increase St. Anthony's desire to love and serve God.

St. Anthony, however, could not seem to find a spot that was isolated enough, for he had many followers. Even at the age of 18, when he moved into the desert spontaneously, numerous people followed. As word of his temptations spread, people would come to him for advice, depriving him of his precious solitude with the Lord. He desired to be alone with God so much that he spent some time living in a closed tomb, depending on some local villagers to bring him food when he was in need. When the tomb was no longer sufficient, he moved into an abandoned Roman fort, only speaking a few words to those who brought him his food and passed it through a hole in the wall. Although he spent much of his life living alone, St. Anthony of the Desert is known as the Father of Cenobitic life, or put more simply, living life according to a rule. St. Anthony helped to organize the people that followed him into the desert into communities united by a common rule. More than a simple "do this, don't do this" rule, **the monastic rule is a way of life and helps to unite people with a common goal.** The communities that St. Anthony helped to establish became more and more common and the people began to form monasteries where they could live apart from society. It was in these monasteries that Western Civilization was preserved and protected.

ST. BENEDICT

You can say that St. Benedict is the most well-known saint associated with the monastic life. He is known as the Father of Western Monasticism, which, like many other things, is different than Eastern Monasticism (thanks Barbarians). St. Benedict was similar to St. Anthony in that he wanted to live his life as a hermit, worshipping God in solitude and offering up the sacrifice of that solitude as a prayer for the rest of the world. And like St. Anthony, he was often tempted by Satan to sin. Once, when he was tempted to lust, he jumped into a thorn bush to remove the temptation. And still like St. Anthony, many people came to him asking him for guidance. In fact, many people came to him and asked him to come and be the leader of their monastery.

Eventually, St. Benedict gave in and agreed to lead the monastery, but he warned those living there that he was very strict and that they probably would not like him. As it turned out, he was right. Within months the people living in the monastery began to complain about his strictness and tried to figure out how to get rid of him. Their solution was simple: instead of just asking him to leave, poison him (cause you know, that's the easiest way to communicate your complaints). And so, they prepared a pitcher of poisoned wine for him to drink from at dinner. When it came time to eat, St. Benedict blessed the food and as he blessed the wine, the pitcher miraculously exploded and the wine was spilled.

Eventually he left the monastery and returned to the wilderness, to a life of prayer and solitude. People, however, kept coming to him, and eventually St. Benedict set out on a new journey: to establish monasteries. He did this with incredible success, establishing twelve monasteries throughout his lifetime.

St. Benedict's great legacy is not just these great monasteries. As Jenga has taught us all, buildings tend to fall down. St. Benedict's legacy will last forever because he really defined a new type of monasticism. He encouraged and built a strong foundation for the monastic life. Prior to St. Benedict, monasticism involved seclusion and isolation to lead a life of prayer. St. Benedict developed a model of "prayer and work" in the monasteries. He made sure that those in his communities didn't focus solely on prayer, but also devoted themselves to some type of work. The monks became farmers, wine-makers, teachers, bookmakers, and the like because St. Benedict taught them that they could *make work holy by making that work a prayer.* He called this the "sanctification of work." We can learn a lot from St. Benedict's example. Whether it's making your bed, or doing the dishes, or taking out the trash, we can offer our work as a prayer.

It was St. Benedict's motto of "Prayer and Work" that saved Western Civilization when the Germanic tribes invaded and divided the West. As the tribes conquered more and more territory and brought their culture of violence and conquest, there was less incentive to create learning and culture. It was in the monasteries that the monks preserved and painstakingly copied ancient texts that were important to them – an incredible labor of love that preserved some of the most important texts of the Western world.

Without the monasteries, the Fall of Rome would have caused much more damage than it did. The knowledge and discoveries of the West probably would have been lost forever. *But in His typical style, God managed to bring something good out of something tragic.* Out of the darkness of Western Europe emerged great saints in the Church, saints like St. Benedict who forever changed our understanding of what it means to "work."

The Monastic movement was one of the primary ways that the Holy Spirit helped the Church to make the transition from being connected to the Roman Empire to being surrounded by Barbarian tribes. This was a dramatic shift and one which nobody saw coming. People expected the Roman Empire to last forever, so when it fell, it took a lot of people by surprise, the Church included. So, the Church could no longer count on the emperors and the spread of the Empire to help spread the message of Jesus Christ. She had to adapt. And only the grace of the Holy Spirit made this possible.

REFLECTION QUESTIONS:

1. What is the benefit of living in solitude as these early saints lived? What can your spiritual life gain from time away from the world? Take 30 minutes today to pray in silence, isolated from the outside world.

2. What does it mean to make your work holy?

3. Where in your life can you do as St. Benedict commissioned and make your work your prayer?

5

CHANGE IS HARD
– THE RISE OF CHRISTENDOM –

Change is hard.

I learned this lesson when I was about 15 years old. That winter, my family and I went to the mountains as we always did. Until then, I had always been a skier (don't hold it against me), but that year my family convinced me to switch over to snowboarding. So, I rented a snowboard and headed up the mountain ready to have fun learning something new. I was not prepared for how hard it would be to learn to snowboard. I spent so much time breaking my fall with my hands that I had to change my waterproof gloves three times. Let's just say, if my hands hadn't been so cold I would have written an angry email to whoever called those gloves "waterproof." Little changes are sometimes as hard as big changes. We all have to go through it, and the Church is no exception.

This was an incredibly difficult lesson for the Church to learn at this time. She had grown so used to operating within the Roman Empire. In fact, in 381 AD, Christianity became the official religion of the Empire. But now, she had none of those benefits, none of that protection. But the Church still had a mission to accomplish, namely, spreading the message of Jesus to all people. And so the Church set out to preach the Gospel to these Barbarian tribes. Think about that for a minute. Think about the horrifying forms of "justice" that took place in these tribes that we talked about in the last chapter. If that was considered right and just, I am terrified about what they considered to be the punishment. Could you find the strength to evangelize someone like that? I think it would be incredibly difficult to say to myself, "They just need Jesus. I'll go tell them about Him and everything He has done for them." And yet this is what the Church did.

In the Nicene Creed we profess belief in "one, holy, catholic and apostolic Church." That the Church is "catholic" means that it is universal, or meant for all people. Today we see this being lived out in the Church's teaching of love and acceptance of all people regardless of race, gender, wealth, or past. The same was true of the Church in the fifth century. Catholics took on the daunting and seemingly impossible task of becoming the unifying principle of all of the Barbarian tribes. Today, that would be like calling a summit of all of the gangs in the Unites States and trying to get them to have one thing in common: love for Jesus Christ. By the grace of the Holy Spirit, the Church was fairly successful, and the result was Christendom, a system in which the Church allied itself with "the state," or in this case, the different secular kings and rulers.

POPE LEO I

As a result of her desire to reunite the West, the Church began to be more involved in politics. Yes, politics (there was no such thing as the "separation of church and state" as we know it today). Popes began to act more like kings, not because they wanted to, but because it was necessary. If there was no central authority, then the West would devolve more than it already had. This movement in the Church began even before the Fall of Rome with Pope Leo I, who was pope from 440 AD to 461 AD. As Leo saw the Empire collapsing he moved to strengthen the Church. He spoke out strongly against heresies and sent out missionaries to continue the process of evangelization. In Rome, he took on more authority because after Rome was sacked in 410 AD, the rulers were very weak.

In fact, in the year 452 AD, Pope Leo saved the city of Rome and its inhabitants. In that year, Attila the Hun, moved to attack Rome because he recognized that the city was vulnerable. Pope Leo, rather than depending upon the emperor and his forces, went out on his own to meet with Attila. This took serious guts. Attila was seen as a savage, he killed without mercy, and was virtually undefeatable in battle. People called him the "scourge of God." The pope did not send someone else as a king might have, but went and met with Attila face to face and tried to reason with him. It seems that Attila must have respected the gesture because, although we don't know exactly what was said, Attila chose not to destroy Rome. This is how it was recorded by the Christian historian Prosper in the year 455 AD in his work entitled "Epitoma Chronicon:"

> Now Attila, having once more collected his forces which had been scattered in Gaul [at the battle of Chalons], took his way through Pannonia into Italy... To the emperor and the senate and Roman people none of all the proposed plans to oppose the enemy seemed so practicable as to send legates to the most savage king and beg for peace. Our most blessed Pope Leo – trusting in the help of God, who never fails the righteous in their trials – undertook the task, accompanied by Avienus, a man of consular rank, and the prefect Trygetius. And the outcome was what his faith had foreseen; for when the king had received the embassy, he was so impressed by the presence of the high priest that he ordered his army to give up warfare and, after he had promised peace, he departed beyond the Danube.

This Church's entrance onto the stage of the Feudal System continued after the death of Pope Leo the Great. Clovis, a powerful and ruthless military leader, was one of the most influential rulers of his day. A pagan for most of his life, Clovis was married to a Christian woman who constantly annoyed him by telling him that his paganism was wrong. Eventually she wore him down and in the year 496 AD Clovis converted to Christianity. Although his conversion occurred in a rather unconventional way, Clovis came to see the beauty of the Church. He told his men not to loot churches in the lands that they conquered, he gave to poor, and even sent generous donations to churches named after his favorite saints. With his conversion, one of the greatest military powers of the fifth century was, at least in name, Catholic. Although it was very imperfect, the Church now had a bond with a secular leader, and a powerful one at that.

POPE GREGORY THE GREAT

As great as the conversion of Clovis was, it was not enough for the Church to unite the West into Christendom. So, the popes continued to emphasize missionary efforts in the lands of the Germanic tribes to bring them the Gospel message of Jesus Christ and to convert them to Christianity. This was of special importance to Pope Gregory the Great, who was pope from 590-604 AD. Pope Gregory is interesting for a multitude of reasons, the chief of which is probably because he was reluctant to be pope and, at least for the first few years of his papacy, basically hated his new job. Pope Gregory was the first pope to have once been a monk. Gregory worked outside of the monastery before, but his heart longed for the quiet life of monasticism. When his predecessor died in 590 AD, however, Gregory was elected the new pope by popular acclamation. Essentially, he had done such a good job when he was outside the monastery that he became very well liked and everyone wanted him to be the next pope. He spent the first few years of his papacy writing about how much he hated being pope (talk about irony). He felt too much of a burden on his shoulders and too much responsibility. But the thing that he disliked the most was that he was not able to live a life of quiet prayer. With the dislike of his new role, it would make sense that he wouldn't live it well, but the opposite is true. In fact, Pope Gregory did such a good job that he today is known as St. Gregory the Great.

So what did he do that was so great? One of Pope Gregory's greatest achievements was his reform of the Mass. Although the parts of the Mass have been the same since the earliest days of the Church, they have not always been in that order. Today, the Mass is arranged very closely to how Pope Gregory assigned them, as well as the inclusion of Gregorian Chant into the liturgy.

Gregorian Chant is a simple method of singing prayers that today is used almost exclusively in the Catholic Church. The addition of music into the prayer of the Church was a game-changer. It is one thing to simply recite words; it adds a new level of beauty to sing them. Think about the lyrics to your favorite song, maybe Taylor Swift's "Shake it Off," or One Direction's "What Makes You Beautiful," or better yet, Matt Maher's "Christ is Risen." Sure, you could just *read* the words and they would still be good. But when you add the element of *singing*, the message becomes much more powerful.

Perhaps the most genius element of Gregorian Chant is its simplicity. You don't have to be a great singer to be able to participate, which is great news for people like me. Gregorian Chant is a beautiful form of music and prayer.

But St. Gregory's influence and importance extended beyond the Mass. Despite not wanting to be pope, he wrote more than any other pope before him. Many of his writings still exist and give us an insight into the life of the Church during the sixth century. One of the coolest things he did was use the term "the Servant of the Servants of God" for himself. It really shows us how humble St. Gregory was and what he envisioned the role of the pope should be. And he shows us a great spiritual truth here. When we look at the Church today we tend to think in terms of a hierarchy like any country or business has. We think of the pope as the CEO or president, the bishops as the board of directors or the congressmen, the priests as managers or mayors, and then finally there is us, the regular people. And while this isn't the worst way to look at the Church, *St. Gregory tells us that the spiritual hierarchy of the Church is different than the physical one.* St. Gregory says that the pope is the servant of the servants of God. The servants of God are really all of us; we all serve God in some way. St. Gregory says that it is the role of the pope to serve the people, not the people to serve the pope.

St. Gregory strengthened the papacy by sending missionaries to far away lands to preach the Gospel message. And it wasn't just Pope Gregory who did this, all of the popes did. And these missionaries had some incredible stories. By putting people into relationship with Jesus Christ, the popes were able to unite more and more people. This unity gave the popes more and more influence when it came to political matters, and in this way the Church, by the grace of the Holy Spirit, managed to survive the Fall of Rome and begin to look to the future.

REFLECTION QUESTIONS:

1. Is change easy or difficult for you? Why?

2. Have you ever been wrong and needed to admit it later on? What makes it so hard to admit when we are wrong?

3. Challenge: Look up Gregorian Chant online and listen to it. The next time you go to pray, use this music as a meditative background.

6

A NEW RELIGION RISES
- THE RISE OF ISLAM -

We've talked a lot about what the Church has been through already. We have covered almost six hundred years of history in just a few short chapters. And in the last few chapters we talked about how the Holy Spirit helped the Church enter a new age, one without the Roman Empire in the West. Until now, we haven't really touched on any controversy. That's about to change because we need to talk about Islam. The rise and spread of Islam had a great impact on Christians, on the Church, and on history.

THE RISE OF ISLAM

During the seventh century, a new religion emerged and spread quickly throughout the world. Since that time, Islam has helped to mold the world as we know it. Now, I am sure that you have heard of Islam. Unfortunately, you have probably heard of Islam in terms of war and violence and *jihad*. While there exist some Muslims who use violence to further their cause, the vast majority of Muslims do not, and there are many things that Christians and Muslims have in common.

So how did Islam come to exist? A man named Muhammad was born around the year 570 AD and lived in the city of Mecca (modern day Saudi Arabia). He spent much of his life as a merchant, and at the beginning of the seventh century, he believed he received visions of the Archangel Gabriel. He claimed to receive these visions from God and wrote down everything he heard from the angel. We know this recording today as the Koran. The Koran claims to be a literal transcript of everything that God said to Muhammad through Gabriel. The Bible, on the other hand, is God's Word mediated through human authors through Divine Inspiration.

The Arabic people were traditionally polytheistic, and Muhammad was no different. So when he began having these visions he must have been genuinely surprised and taken back by the idea of one Supreme God. Muhammad, however, was convinced of the authenticity of these visions and began to teach others about this One True God. He claimed to be a prophet in the same line as Jesus and Moses and gained a small following. Muhammad's teachings eventually upset the polytheistic culture of Mecca and he was forced to flee in order to escape the anger of some of the Arabic tribes. Muhammad and his followers fled to the city of Medina where Muhammad became both a spiritual and military leader.

For the next 100 years, Muslims waged war against the surrounding Arabic tribes, even daring to engage in battle with the mighty Byzantine Empire – the Eastern half of the Roman Empire. By the year 750 AD, Muhammad's religion had spread from the small city of Medina, across Northern Africa, and even into Spain. *No other religion, except Christianity, had ever spread so quickly.*

There were three major reasons that Islam spread so quickly:

1. *Culture*
In polytheistic cultures, if your tribe was conquered by another it meant that your gods had also been conquered by their gods, and therefore your tribe should worship those gods. So, whenever Muslims waged war against a tribe and conquered them, many of the members of that tribe adopted worship of "the God of the Muslims."

2. *Simplicity*
Remember all of those heresies from a previous chapter? Those were not so simple. In fact, at times the difference between the right belief and the heresy was a single Greek letter. Almost like a really awful spelling bee. It could be very difficult to remember exactly what Christians believed. Islam however, did not have a deep theology because they did not need one. Muslims view God as a master to be obeyed and so they don't have a real need to understand Him. In fact, "Islam" means submission and "Muslim"

means one who submits. Islam itself can be summed up by its Five Major Pillars.

First Pillar – Belief or *Iman:* This is a profession of belief that all Muslims make: "There is no god but God, and Muhammad is his prophet." It can be compared to the Apostle's or Nicene Creed. It is, however, far shorter. This is Muslim theology in its most simple form. To convert to Islam, one makes this simple profession. There doesn't need to be any other rites or rituals.

Second Pillar – Worship or *Salat:* Muslim prayer is highly ritualized. Every day, five times a day, facing the direction of Mecca, Muslims recite specific words while assuming specific postures of prayer. Salat, you can say, is similar to the "Liturgy of the Hours" or the "Divine Office" which Christians all over the world pray at specific times of the day.

Third Pillar – Fasting or *Sawm:* During the 9th month of the lunar calendar Muslims celebrate Ramadan. During this time, Muslims fast from food and drink from sun up until sun down. As you might be aware, Catholics fast during the liturgical season of Lent. What you may not know is Catholics are also called make some form of fast or sacrifice on every Friday of the year, not just the ones during Lent.

Fouth Pillar – Almsgiving or *Zakat:* Muslims are required to give a percentage of their property to the poor each month. As Catholics we call this a tithe.

Fifth Pillar – Pilgrimage or *Hajj:* Muslims must make a pilgrimage to Mecca at least once during their lifetime. As Catholics we also go on pilgrimages to Holy sites, including the Vatican, the tombs of our favorite saints, etc.

For many people at the time of its emergence, Islam made more sense than Christianity. It was less complicated, politicized, and intricate. Following the Five Pillars seemed like a much simpler task.

3. *Taxes*
Jizya was a tax that any non-Muslim who was living in an area controlled by the Muslims had to pay. It was essentially a "non-conversion" tax. If a Christian or a Jew wanted to keep their faith, they had to pay this tax. Sometimes it was a reasonable price, and sometimes it was an unreasonable price. Either way, it was a form

of discrimination and it was definitely a motivator for many to convert to Islam just so that they could live in peace.

Although these reasons were certainly influential, we must not discount the numerous people who had an authentic conversion to Islam. As with all religions, there is a sense of beauty and of truth in Islam, and many who saw that beauty would have been attracted to it. Unfortunately, there are many today who fail to glimpse that beauty and would write-off all Muslims as vicious and violent terrorists. The reality is that the vast majority of Muslims condemn the actions of those men just as much as we do.

In fact, many Muslims are more faithful to their religion than we as Christians are to our own. How many of us pray five times a day or are willing to pray in public? How many of us truly give of our time and our talents to build up the Church? How often do we really challenge ourselves to grow spiritually during the season of Lent? There is a lot that we as Christians can learn from Muslims, and I think there is also a lot that we can teach them about a God who loves us and makes us His sons and daughters. But this learning and teaching can only happen if we leave our prejudice and judgments behind and begin to love and respect one another.

Now if you have a general understanding of history, you might think that the next topic we should talk about is the Crusades. The Crusades were the biggest conflict between Christians and Muslims. But before we can talk about the Crusades, we have to talk about the Great Schism because it greatly affected the Crusades.

REFLECTION QUESTIONS:

1. What are some misconceptions you have about Muslims?

2. Have you experienced a time in your life that differences have held you back from getting along with someone else? What is it that held you back?

3. This chapter shows us that Christians and Muslims are actually more alike than we may think, what is it that we can learn from each other?

4. How can we incorporate this new knowledge into our daily encounters with those of other faiths and beliefs?

7

LIKE A REALLY BAD BREAKUP
- THE GREAT SCHISM -

One of my favorite things about being Catholic is that (for the most part) we don't have to choose between two things. There is this silly saying that "You can't have your cake and eat it too." As Catholics that rule doesn't really apply to us. Jesus isn't human or divine, He is both! The Church isn't perfect or imperfect; the Church is both! Now, before you throw this book in the trash and call me a lunatic, let me explain. The Church is perfect because she was established by Jesus Himself. He created the Church and He doesn't create anything that is imperfect. Even more than that though, the Church is perfect because the Church is the body of Christ (Romans 12:5). And if this image freaks you out a little bit that's a good thing, because if we are members of the Body of Christ then we have a very specific role to play in the Church, and that is a lot of responsibility.

On the other hand, the Church is also imperfect because all of her members are imperfect – there is no perfect Catholic. And as members of the Church, we often mess up and do things we are not proud of, or at least, shouldn't be proud of. **But sinful men who do sinful things do not make the Church bad, or hypocritical.** More than anything, I would say that people doing bad things highlights why we need the Church. If we are so prone to doing terrible things, how can we ever expect to do something good? The answer is grace, and grace comes to us from Christ through the Church. And grace was majorly needed in 1054 AD when some really good men made some really bad decisions.

In 1054 AD, the Catholic Church fragmented in two: the Latin or Roman Rite and the Eastern Rite. This separation didn't just happen overnight, though. The tensions had been building up for centuries. It was like any big break-up. First she texts him too often, then he doesn't talk to her enough, and next thing you know they are both miserable without the other.

THE FIRST TENSION

The tensions that led up the Great Schism really started in the third century during the reign of Emperor Diocletian. During his reign he split the Roman Empire into four governing districts to make it easier to control. But because they were split into different districts, each district began establishing its own subculture with its own special way of doing things. In a small way, we see this in the United States. In some places, people call soda "pop." In other places, people call every soda "coke." In the south they say "y'all" when speaking to multiple people, but in Pittsburgh they say "yinz." And no, that doesn't make any sense. The point is, although soda is still soda, different regions develop different traditions involving it. The same thing happened with the Church in the different districts of Rome. The Christians in the two Eastern Districts began doing things a little differently than the Christians in the two western districts and we began to see some distinction between the two different forms of worship.

These differences turned into tensions when, in the year 330 AD, Emperor Constantine moved the capitol of the Roman Empire from Rome to the city of Byzantium, which he renamed Constantinople—because lets be honest, we would all name a city after ourselves if we had the chance. Rome was in the Western half of the Empire while Constantinople was in the Eastern half. With this move, the Eastern half of the Empire began to grow in prosperity and wealth, while the Western half began to decline, and then was invaded by the Barbarians, like we mentioned earlier. As the economic and political power shifted more and more to the East, the Bishops in the East thought that the religious authority should shift to the East as well. The Bishop of Rome, however, as the successor of Peter, remained pope and this created more tensions between Christians in the East and West.

THE SECOND TENSION

These political tensions, though, were just the icing on the cake. Ultimately, the theological tensions were a much bigger deal than the political ones. The theological tensions really began in the year 589 AD when the Council of Toledo introduced a new phrase into the Nicene Creed. This phrase is known as the *filioque* clause.

The *filioque* clause is a group of three words that today are part of the Nicene Creed that we as Roman Catholics recite. Which three words, you ask? "And the Son." Yup, those three words have caused more suffering and strife than we could ever imagine. To many, this phrase may not seem that important, and you might have said these words every Sunday at Mass without even thinking about them or even recognizing their existence, but for others these words could not be more crucial. Before 589 AD, the Nicene Creed said that Catholics believe in "the Holy Spirit, the Lord and giver of life, who proceeds from the father, who with the Father and Son together is adored and glorified, who has spoken through the prophets." Now hopefully that sounds familiar, because it is almost word for word what we proclaim at Mass on Sundays. Almost. The Third Council of Toledo changed the language of this part of the Creed to say that Catholics believe in "the Holy Spirit, the Lord and giver of life, who proceeds from the Father **and the Son**, who with the Father and Son together is adored and glorified, who has spoken through the prophets."

This phrase was added as a way to clarify that the Church believed and taught that the Holy Spirit emanates, or proceeds from, both the Father and the Son. Remember, its important to know the truth about who God is so that we can love Him as much as possible, and there were many people who were beginning to believe and teach that the Holy Spirit proceeded only from the Father. If this were true, however, it would imply that the Father was greater than the Son and the Holy Spirit, rather than equal to them, which is not true. Many members of the Church believed that it was necessary to include this phrase in the Creed in order to clarify the Church's teaching on the Holy Trinity. But for others, including this statement in the Creed violated the Church's claim that the Creed would not change. As you probably already know, the Church chose to include the words "and the Son" so that the teachings on the Trinity would be as clear as possible. As it is, teaching about the Trinity is hard enough, but at least now the Church has a clear teaching on the place of the Holy Spirit within the Trinity. After this addition, many were concerned about whether or not this teaching was even correct. But in the year 1014 AD, Pope Benedict VIII essentially proclaimed it to be true by reciting it at Mass. From that moment on, the controversy has been not so much about whether it is true or not, but instead about the pope's authority to include it in the Creed.

THE THIRD TENSION

The authority of the pope became the final sticking point between the East and West. It was the straw that broke the camel's back. Remember, Eastern Rite Catholics felt as if the authority of the Church should be moving toward the East, toward the place where the economy was thriving. They thought that the authority of the pope should be decreasing and the authority of the patriarchs, who are essentially the archbishops of the major territories of the Church in the East, should be increasing. They resented the fact that Rome, despite having virtually no political or economic influence, continued to exert such a great spiritual influence. And perhaps we have seen this type of resentment in our own lives. Have you ever been jealous of someone because of their role or position? Maybe you play a sport and there is someone playing a position that you could play better. Or maybe you have been in a school play or musical and someone who you don't think is very talented got the lead role. The point is that our human pride tends to make us jealous of others when we view them as less deserving than ourselves and we begin to covet what they have.

All of these tensions boiled over in the year 1054 AD when the pope and the Patriarch of Constantinople tried to excommunicate each other. And in a terribly ironic way that is typical of God's sense of humor, it was all a giant misunderstanding, but the damage was done and the Church was split. In 1053 AD, a cardinal by the name of Humbert was sent to the East to excommunicate the Patriarch of Constantinople, Michael Cerularius. Patriarch Cerularius was very opposed to many of the practices in the Western Church and so he closed many of the Latin rite churches in the East. By the time Humbert got to Constantinople though, Pope Leo IX had died, which meant he didn't have the authority to excommunicate anyone. Without cell phones, Twitter, or Snapchat, though, Cardinal Humbert was entirely unaware that Pope Leo IX had died and thus delivered the excommunication anyway. Upon finding out that he had been excommunicated, the Patriarch was understandably upset and in return he declared Pope Leo IX, who was now dead, excommunicated. And then in dramatic fashion, he burned the statement of excommunication that had been delivered to him.

To this day, the Schism continues to exist. There is still a difference between Eastern and Western Rites in the Church. Perhaps the biggest difference between the two is the understanding of the role of the pope. For Western Rite Catholics, the pope is the successor of St. Peter and therefore the leader of all of the successors of the other Apostles, the bishops (Matthew 16:18). The pope is the head of the Church, and has authority over the whole Church. However, for many Eastern Rite Catholics the pope does not have authority over the other bishops. Instead he is as seen as having an honorary title as the "first among equals."

In more recent history there have been great strides in bringing an end to this schism. Through prayer and dialogue, many of the individual Eastern churches have once again accepted the authority of the pope. As Catholics we know and believe that Jesus desires His Church to be united (John 17:20-21). And yet, here is the Church established by Jesus Himself divided. It is our job to work for this unity, especially through prayer. So let us begin today to pray for an end to this schism, to offer the Mass for the unity of Catholics – and Christians – everywhere, so that God's will can be more perfectly established here on Earth.

REFLECTION QUESTIONS:

1. Has a misunderstanding ever gotten out of hand in your life and caused big problems? What led to the misunderstanding?

2. Who do you need to be reconciled with? What steps do you need to take toward reconciliation?

3. Challenge: For the next week, make it a point to pray for unity within the Christian Church every day.

8

JERUSALEM, OUR HOME
- THE CRUSADES -

When I was little, there was a rule about not playing ball in the house. It was a rule that, despite its simplicity, we just couldn't seem to follow. And, sure enough, the day soon came that we broke my mom's nice collector plates because we were playing ball in the house. My first instinct was to fix them. Grabbing my Elmer's glue from my backpack I set about frantically trying to glue the plates back together, to no avail. And when my mom got home, there I sat, surrounded by broken plates and covered in glue, crying. I wonder if this is what Pope Urban felt like after the Crusades. But, I'm getting ahead of myself. Let's backtrack a little bit.

As Islam spread from Medina it became almost inevitable that there would be some sort of clash between this new Muslim Empire and the Christian Byzantine Empire (remember, Christianity became the legal religion of the Empire in 380 AD). Muslims conquered Jerusalem and the surrounding areas. They imposed the jizya (taxes) on those Christians who would not leave their homes, mistreated Christian pilgrims who were on their way to visit the Holy Land, and even went so far as to kill some Christians. This was obviously upsetting for many Christians, especially because Jerusalem and the cities surrounding it were the places where Jesus lived, died, and rose from the grave. It was here that Christians could go and pray at the tomb of Jesus, or place their hand in the hole where His cross was raised. **These were the tensions that helped lead to (wait for it... dramatic music)... The Crusades.**

In its most simple definition: The Crusades were a series of wars that were waged with the intent of regaining control over Jerusalem and the land around it. Depending on who you ask, you will hear that there were anywhere from seven to nine major crusades and numerous minor ones. How hard can it be to count them? Well, there is a reason that we are historians and not mathematicians. The First Crusade began in the year 1095 AD and ultimately was the only Crusade that succeeded. The last Crusade ended in the year 1291 with the defeat of the Christian army.

The Crusades are often brought up as an example of the evils of religion. People will say things like, "How good can religion be? Look how many wars it has caused!" The Crusades are also occasionally brought up when people want to tell you that Christianity is really hypocrisy and that you shouldn't be a Christian. However, neither of these claims is actually supported when we look at the Crusades. **Since the year 2000, there has been plenty of research and writings concluding that religion serves as a cause for a very small percentage of wars.** One of my favorites is the *Encyclopedia of Wars*. Published in 2004, it states that only 7% of wars were caused by religion. The study goes on further to say that of those 7%, almost half can be traced to Islam. It is easy to **claim** that religion and Christianity are the primary cause of war, but it is **impossible** to prove because it is just not true.

Okay, so Christianity isn't as evil as some people claim it is. But, that doesn't mean that Christians haven't done some terrible things throughout history. We may claim Jesus Christ as our role-model, but we are still human. We are flawed and sinful and we make plenty of mistakes. So, if the Crusades are not as bad as they are often portrayed, how should we understand them? Like this: **The Crusades were a series of wars intended to regain control of the Holy Land for Christianity in which both sides committed atrocities because they are human.**

THE ORIGINAL AIM

In the year 1071 AD, the Seljuk Turks captured the Holy Land from the Egyptians. The Seljuk Turks were far less tolerant of other religious beliefs than their predecessors in the Holy Land so the persecution of Christians living there got much worse. The Turks started a campaign to conquer the Byzantine Empire, and in that same year defeated the Byzantine Army soundly at the Battle of Manzikert. After this battle, the Byzantine Army and Empire was almost defenseless.

Maybe it was pride or ego, or maybe it was a lingering distrust after the very recent Great Schism, but the emperor in the East didn't immediately ask for help. In fact, he waited over 20 years! Finally, Emperor Alexios asked Pope Urban II to send aid. Pope Urban convened the Council of Clermont and asked people to travel east and defend the Empire. Apparently, Pope Urban was also a multi-tasker because he also **saw this as an opportunity to re-unite Christianity (East and West) and take back the Holy Land.** So, instead of just telling the Christians in the West to defend the Byzantine Empire, he called on them to re-establish the pilgrimage routes to Jerusalem. In doing so, he assured that Christians would help defend the Eastern Empire and continue on to capture the Holy City.

Now, some people claim those who went on Crusades did so in an attempt to get wealthy or because they were bloodthirsty, rather than going because of their faith. This claim would certainly fit the narrative of evil Christians under the control of a corrupt pope trying to take over the world. In reality, however, *this is almost exactly the opposite of what was happening.*

THE FIRST CRUSADE

The pope called on Christians to go to the aid of the Church in the East. They weren't promised any money or any glory, only that God would be with them. In fact, almost all of the sermons used to convince people to go on Crusades talked about the difficulty of the journey to the East and the certain trials the Crusaders would face. These sermons were like really terrible recruiting speeches for the Army; instead of glorifying battle and talking about heroics, the sermons spoke honestly about the brutality of war, making sure that soldiers knew what they were getting into. As the Crusaders marched toward Jerusalem, they captured major cities along the way. One of those cities was called Antioch. If you want to see the depth of the Crusaders' faith, look no further than this city.

The Crusaders captured the city of Antioch on June 2, 1098 after a seven-month siege. Exhausted after months of battle, they went into the city to rest, resupply, and prepare for the next part of their journey. Unfortunately for the Crusaders, they remained at Antioch for far too long. Just five days later, a new Muslim force arrived and began to lay siege to the city, just as the Crusaders had done for the past seven months. If this were any other time, the Crusaders could have held out in the city for months. They would have had plenty of food, water, and supplies. But the Muslims who had held the city for the past seven months had eaten all of the food and used up most of the water. Not only that, but the seven month siege had done much damage to the city, and many of the Crusaders were tired and injured. As the Muslims laid siege to Antioch, the Crusaders became desperate. Short on food they were forced to eat their own horses to survive. Horses. They ate horses. I don't think you could pay me to do that. Anyway, as the situation became more and more desperate, it seemed as if the Crusaders would need a miracle to survive the siege and make it to Jerusalem. And a miracle is what they got.

A priest named Peter Bartholomew came to leaders of the Crusading armies and told them that he had a vision in which St. Andrew told him where the lance was that was used to pierce the side of Jesus as He hung on the Cross (John 19:34). Peter took them to the Cathedral of St. Peter and showed them where to dig, and there, just a few feet below the surface of the ground was a spear. Now the authenticity of the spear can be debated. In fact, there was a spear in Constantinople that people claimed was the Holy Lance. *What cannot be debated is the effect that this discovery had on the Crusaders.* The Crusaders, desperate and despairing, at once had their spirits lifted! The discovery of the spear gave them hope that God really was on their side and would deliver them. Peter Bartholomew also reported a vision commanding the Crusaders to fast for five days before they could win the Battle. So these men, who had been starving for weeks, if not months, fasted for five days and then went into battle! I have a hard enough time fasting when I am well-fed, I can't imagine fasting if I was already starving. **The fact that these men were so uplifted by the discovery of the Holy Lance and that they were willing to fast despite their dire circumstances shows us that they really did have a deep faith in God.**

The event at Antioch wasn't even the most dramatic display of faith the Crusaders would make during the First Crusade. Like any good showmen, they saved the best for last. When the Crusaders arrived at Jerusalem in 1099 AD, they put on a show that nobody would ever forget. After a disastrous first attempt to take the city without any siege equipment, it was time, yet again, for a miracle. Without siege equipment, to scale the walls of a city, like siege towers, ladders, rams, catapults, etc. it would have been very difficult, if not impossible, to capture a city. The Muslims in control of the city knew that the Crusaders would need wood to build these things, so before the Crusaders got there they made sure to burn all of the trees in the area. And yet, miraculously, the Crusaders found 400 wooden boards that allowed them to build at least one siege engine. And when reinforcements arrived by ship, the Crusaders took those ships apart and used the wood to build even more siege equipment.

Before they laid siege to the city, however, they did something that was simultaneously incredibly awesome and pretty ludicrous. A priest named Peter Desiderius said that he had a vision in which the recently dead bishop who had led the Crusaders told them to walk around the city barefoot before laying siege to it. And so they did. They put down their weapons, picked up their incense and walked around Jerusalem barefoot, stepping on sharp stones and other rubble. Can you imagine what the Muslims must have thought?! Here are their enemies, preparing for war, by walking around the city barefoot, singing songs, and blowing trumpets. And you know there was at least one Crusader looking at all his friends going, "Guys, seriously? Quit messing around. Come on. Put your shoes back on! This is a war!" What loonies! But if there is one thing I know, it's that you never underestimate the power of crazy.

But was it really crazy? Was it crazy for Joshua to trust God when He commanded him to march around Jericho blowing the trumpets (Joshua 6:1-27)? Is it crazy to trust the command of God instead of the wisdom of man? St. Paul would have said that these were the wisest men of all! He did write to the Corinthians that "God chose what is foolish in the world to shame the wise..." (1 Corinthians 1:27). And, "If any one among you thinks that he is wise in this age, let him become a fool that he may become wise. For the wisdom of this world is folly with God" (1 Corinthians 3:18-19). The Crusaders put their trust in God in a radical way. They trusted him with their life, with the success of the journey they had spent the last four years on. They trusted Him with boldness.

When was the last time you trusted God in this way? When did you last commit yourself to God and say, "Your will be done, Lord" (Luke 22:42)? When did you last pray as John the Baptist saying, "I must decrease, He must increase" (John 3:30)? Take a minute right now and ask yourself these questions honestly. If we are going to really follow God's will for our lives, really trust Him, we must be willing to make fools of ourselves. We cannot be afraid of stepping out in faith and being mocked by others. Yes, we must too use our ability to reason. God gave you that gift, well, for a reason! But, when God calls us to action we have to be ready to act, even if the consequences include losing our "street cred."

The Crusaders, though many were devout Christians, still had their faults. Throughout the course of the long journey to Jerusalem it was not uncommon for soldiers to attack small villages or caravans for supplies, harming innocent people in the process. In 1099 AD, when they entered and conquered Jerusalem, the Crusaders massacred Jews and Muslims alike who had fought against them. We could go on an on looking at the injustices that the Crusaders committed, but let's look at the big one: the Fourth Crusade.

THE FOURTH CRUSADE

During the Fourth Crusade, the Crusaders attacked the city of Zara, which was inhabited and controlled by Christians, and then they proceeded to Constantinople, the capitol of the Eastern Empire. It was in Constantinople that the Crusaders were supposed to prepare themselves to try to recapture the Holy Land. Apparently though, that was not communicated. Instead of meeting up with the Byzantine Army and leaving for Jerusalem, the Crusaders attacked the city of Constantinople. They pillaged the city, set fires, stole wealth, killed innocent people, and then began the long return journey home. Yeah, a far cry from Church teaching, huh? All of these things happened without her approval, and in fact the Church even went so far as to excommunicate those who participated in attacking the cities of Zara and Constantinople. The Fourth Crusade was supposed to be an opportunity for Christians in the West to help those in the East, and to help reunite East and West as Pope Urban II had wanted, but it quickly became a catastrophe. In fact, many historians will argue that the actions of the Crusaders in Constantinople did so much damage to the city that the fall of Constantinople to the Ottoman Empire in 1453 became inevitable.

The attack on Constantinople made the Great Schism more real. It drove East and West further apart than they already were. Just imagine if the United States was attacked in California, so Florida sent troops to help California. But instead of helping, the Floridian soldiers attacked the city of Sacramento, stole all of the money in the banks, set buildings on fire, broke into people's houses and stole their valuables, then turned around and went home. Obviously Californians would be upset. They would be upset and probably wouldn't trust those Floridians for a while (but who really trusts people who live near alligators anyway?).

Although there were many terrible things that happened during the Crusades, it is important to remember that these events were in no way ordered or approved of by the pope or the Church. The people doing the fighting were just as human as you and I. Have you ever been really upset and that rage caused you to kill someone? No? Oh. In that case, me neither. What about angry enough to do something you later regretted? I think most of can relate to that.

The one thing we often ignore when we look at the atrocities committed by the Crusaders is the fact that they were at war. Although I have never been in a war, I can imagine that the emotional stress can make you act in ways that you never imagined possible. No, not everything is fair in war, and not all actions can be justified. But, the Crusaders actions are understandable. It can be easy to understand how men who haven't seen their families in years, who are half-starved, incredibly dehydrated, sick of constantly being attacked, and angered by the deaths of their friends could vent some frustration and anger against those they perceived as their enemies. In fact, if you look at virtually any war in history you can easily find some atrocities committed by the soldiers of one side or the other. Should they have known better? Yes. Was it wrong? Yes. Do I understand why they did it? Only as much as I can imagine it, which can't be very much because I have never been at war. Can we hold the Church responsible for the actions of these soldiers? Absolutely not.

Ultimately, when we look at the Crusades we see the problem of good intentions mixed with sinful humanity. Even when we set out on the path to do something good, we can often go off of that path and do something bad. The Crusaders set off to re-capture the Holy Land for Christianity and to make it safe to travel there again, and in the end they failed. But that doesn't mean that their intentions were not good, it just means that they were human and capable of messing up. Today, the violence around the Holy Land takes a different form. Tragically, there are still people dying over the right to "own" the Holy Land. **So today, let us begin a new Crusade. Not one of violence and bloodshed, but one of prayer.** Let us pray that the Prince of Peace would conquer all of the conflicted hearts in the world, including our own. May we all come to know the peace that Jesus offers and may we share that peace with others.

REFLECTION QUESTIONS:

1. Have your good intentions ever had negative consequences? Think about what went wrong – what could you do differently so there is a more positive outcome?

2. Many people cite the Crusades as evidence that religion is evil; how would you respond to this argument based on this chapter and your own personal experience?

3. How can you both pray for peace and be an active agent of peace in your life? What three things can you do to bring peace to your life and the lives of those around you?

9

POPES VS. KINGS
– THE AVIGNON PAPACY –

Have you ever heard the phrase, "Out of the frying pan and into the fire"? It's something your grandparents might say to emphasize escaping one difficulty only to find yourself in a more difficult one. Like when Katniss Everdeen escapes the Quarter Quell at the Hunger Games only to find herself at the center of an all out war between the Districts and the Capitol. Or when, at the end of *The Maze Runner,* we discover that Thomas and his friends have escaped the labyrinth only to unknowingly be involved in a "second round" of experiments. Or the way in which Shaggy and Scooby always seem to get away from the monster only to find out he was already in the closet they just hid in. Well, at the end of the Crusades, the Church had an "out of the frying pan and into the fire" moment. Certainly the Crusades were a bad thing, no one would ever deny that. But the Crusades never threatened to destroy the Church. What followed, though, could have undermined everything the Church stands on.

In the year 1305, just nine years after the end of what most consider to be the last Crusade, Pope Clement V moved from Rome to Avignon, France. This seemingly unimportant detail resulted in a rift in the Church that would not be resolved until the 15th century. Just one small move had more than 100 years of consequences (remember that next time you make a "small" decision). So how did this move come about? As with all of history, its complicated.

Beginning in 1294, France and England were at war, and in order to pay for this war they tried to tax the Church by taking a portion of the money that people were donating. Understandably, this upset Pope Boniface VIII. He firmly believed that money donated to the Church should be spent building up the Church, serving the poor, and providing for those in need. This had always been the case, and even today the Church enjoys tax-exempt status as a charitable organization. So when the French and the English began to demand as much as half of the Church's money in their own country, the pope had to respond. And so began one of the greatest, most intricate fights in the history of the Church.

AN UNCLEAR RELATIONSHIP

Unfortunately, the role of the pope and the Church in matters of politics and secular government had not been clearly established yet. During the Crusades, the pope's political influence had grown immensely, but nobody had ever really talked about whether the pope or the king had more authority. So when Pope Boniface VIII said any taxes on the Church had to be pre-approved by the pope and then subsequently made the statement that "God has set popes over kings and kingdoms," it was King Philip of France's turn to be upset. And, because both men were a bit stubborn, and both were convinced they should have more authority than the other, things continued to escalate.

First, King Philip countered the pope's declaration with his own: no money would be exported from France. France was the biggest Catholic state, so Pope Boniface decided that some money was better than no money and allowed the taxation of the clergy.

King Philip continued to defy the pope and looked for ways to undermine him and show his own superiority. Pope Boniface finally had enough, and wrote a letter entitled *"Unam Sanctam"* in which he wrote "God has set popes over kings and kingdoms." King Philip wrote back rather rudely: "Your venerable stupidity may know that we are nobody's vassals in temporal matters." Now that takes guts. I'm not trying to glorify Philip's disobedience, but come on, to call the pope "your venerable stupidness" takes some serious ego. I would never speak to my mother that way, and certainly never the pope. But those words are mild in comparison to what happened next.

Incensed by Philip's arrogance and disobedience, Pope Boniface excommunicated King Philip. This meant that King Philip would no longer be in union with the Church and could not receive the sacraments until he had been forgiven of his sins. What was Philip's response? He sent an army to kidnap Pope Boniface. Yes, you read that right. He kidnapped the pope to try to get him to forgive him his sins. King Philip would stop at nothing to claim power and authority over the Pope. So for three long days, Pope Boniface was beaten, starved, and given no drink. We aren't quite sure why he was released after three days, but it didn't matter much. He could not handle such mistreatment in his old age and died within the month.

You might think that King Philip would reconsider his actions after they resulted in the death of Pope Boniface. I mean, even the most hardened criminals are looking at this situation going, "Woah, bro, things escalated really fast." But King Philip was still not satisfied. In fact, when Pope Boniface's successor, Pope Benedict XI died under suspicious circumstances within a year of his election, many people believed that Philip was in some way responsible. And while we may never know if he really did have anything to do with it, he certainly took advantage of the situation.

After the death of Pope Benedict XI, King Philip began maneuvering to get a man of his choice elected as pope. The only difficulty was that people don't just campaign and try to get elected pope: the College of Cardinals is in charge of the voting. Philip pulled every string possible to get someone he could manipulate to be elected as pope and he eventually succeeded; a French Cardinal, Bertrand de Goth, became Pope Clement V.

Now as much as I don't like King Philip, I have to admit that he was pretty smart. He always seemed to be thinking several moves ahead, anticipating how things would turn out. He knew that if a non-Italian was elected pope, the Italians would go crazy. And sure enough, the election of a French Cardinal as the Successor of St. Peter drove them nuts. Riots broke out. You would've thought that the Italian hockey team had just lost the Stanley Cup or something. If cars had existed, there would have been more than a few flipped over and slowly burning. The newly elected pope had experienced a minor freak out. And who was there to comfort him and offer him safety? That's right, King Philip of France. And so in 1309 Pope Clement V left Rome, and for the next 70 years, the Successor of St. Peter, the Bishop of Rome, resided in Avignon, France.

This 70-year period is, for obvious reasons known as the **Avignon Papacy**. It also goes by a different name, though – The Babylonian

Captivity. This Babylonian Captivity should not be confused with the Babylonian Captivity in the Old Testament in which the Israelites, God's Chosen People, were captured by the Babylonians and taken into slavery. However, this time is known as the Babylonian Captivity because during these 70 years, the Church – the people of God – had, in a sense, been captured by the French King. Pope Clement V was not strong enough to resist King Philip and ended up doing things that he would later regret and were not in the best interests of the Church.

While there were many negative consequences about having the pope in France, two are especially relevant:

1. The first was that Rome began to fall apart. The pope had been the central authority in Rome, and now he was gone. So different people began fighting for power. Rome became very dangerous, and that was one of the reasons the pope didn't return.

2. The second consequence was much more serious for the Church: corruption. The governing body of the Church began to operate much more like a secular government and corruption began to run rampant. People saw the corruption and the influence of the French government and lost faith in the Church and lost trust in the pope.

Now, obviously this is a bad thing. The Church often plays the role of helping us to love one another better. If we don't listen to the Church we can often get caught up living a life that hurts others and ourselves even though it may "feel good" at the time. As the great G.K. Chesterton once put it, "I don't need a Church to tell me I'm wrong when I know I am wrong. I need a Church to tell me I'm wrong when I think I am right." It is the Church's duty to always proclaim Jesus Christ crucified, even though that may be a stumbling block to others, or may appear as foolishness to even more (1 Corinthians 1:23). When we stop listening to the voice of the Church, we stop listening to the words of Jesus.

THE RETURN TO ROME

As time progressed, it became clear to many that the pope belonged back in Rome. This was most clear to a young woman named Catherine who was born in Siena in 1347. Growing up in the home of a wealthy family, Catherine began to have religious visions at a very young age. By the time she was sixteen years old she dedicated her life to the service of others through the model of St. Dominic. As she grew older, people began to recognize her incredible wisdom. Although she never had any formal theological training, she had incredible insights into who God was and how He loved us. In fact, she was so brilliant that today she is one of only four women to have been named a Doctor of the Church – someone whose teaching is recognized in the Church as having been especially important, especially when it comes to Theology or Church Doctrine.

But Catherine was more than a brilliant theologian. She was kind, and compassionate, spending much of her life as a nurse taking care of those with leprosy. And she was about as gutsy as they come. St. Catherine was no quiet, mousy girl. She was passionate and loud, and maybe even a little obnoxious to some. She spoke out against injustices and errors without beating around the bush. While this did make some people not like her, it ultimately worked in her favor, and in the favor of the whole Church because in 1376 she travelled from Italy to Avignon, France to confront the pope.

Confront the pope?! She can't do that! Well, actually she can. And she did. Papal infallibility, or the teaching that the pope cannot err when it comes to issues of faith and morals, is **extremely** limited. It certainly does not apply to **everything** he says and does. One of the things that Catherine thought he was wrong about was residing in Avignon so she went to tell him all about it and to persuade him to come back to Rome. And within the year, Pope Gregory XI moved the papacy back to Rome.

OUT OF THE FRYING PAN AND INTO THE FIRE... AGAIN

Although Pope Gregory XI came back to Rome, he could not live forever. There would come a time when he would no longer be the pope and the cardinals, who after 70 years in France were almost all French, would have to elect his successor. And sure enough, this day came just two years later on March 27, 1378.

Now at this time, it was customary to elect the new pope in the same place that the previous pope had died. So, although most of the cardinals at this time were French, the cardinals convened in Rome to elect the new pope. To satisfy the Italians, and perhaps concerned that an angry, murderous mob might form if they elected another French pope, the cardinals elected Bartolomeo Prignano, who became Pope Urban VI. Pope Urban was quickly disliked by the French cardinals. He made it clear that he was not going to tolerate any corruption and called them out for their lavish lifestyles and their neglect of the Church. No one likes to have their flaws pointed out, especially if the person pointing out those flaws is doing so in an aggressive way. Which is just what Pope Urban did. He made the French cardinals so mad that many left Rome and went back to France. They declared the election of Pope Urban VI invalid claiming that they had been pressured by the Romans to elect him, and then they elected their own "pope," Clement VII.

And now everyone was confused. There were two men, both claiming to be the real pope and both threatening the other with excommunication. Different countries began picking sides, some with Urban VI and Rome, the others with Clement VII and Avignon. Today, when it comes to a matter of official Church teaching, we can just ask the pope. Heck you can tweet him "@Pontifex" if you really wanted to. But since nobody was sure who the real pope was, there wasn't really anyone they could ask. And unfortunately, there was no quick solution. For the next 40 years there were multiple men who claimed to be the real pope at the same time. This is known as the **Western Schism** and is certainly one of the lowest points in the history of the Church. And it would get much worse before it got any better.

How could it get any worse? Well, how about by getting even more confusing. What's more confusing than two popes? Three popes. Three popes is always more confusing than two. But before we get there, recognize again the danger of pride. There was no real theological difference between those who were obedient to Urban or to Clement. But because of their pride, neither group would say that they were wrong, and so the feud continued even after both men had died. Pride and selfishness are at the root of all of our sins. And what is the opposite of pride and selfishness? Selflessness and love.

This is why Jesus said that if we love God perfectly and love others perfectly we will not sin. "On these two commandments [love of God and love of neighbor] depend all the law and the prophets" (Matthew 22:37-40). This same teaching applies to us today: if we love God above all else and love our neighbor for God's sake *in every instance* we will never sin again. Sounds easy, right? Unfortunately, it sounds much easier than it is. It means constantly dying to ourselves and putting others first. It means never again making a choice even for the slightest selfish reason. It is not a life for the faint of heart.

THE PROBLEM IS (FINALLY) SOLVED

In 1409, a council was called in Pisa with the intention of resolving the Western Schism. Unfortunately, the Council of Pisa did exactly the opposite. The cardinals wanted both of the current popes – Pope Boniface IX who succeeded Pope Urban, and anti-pope Benedict XIII – to resign and so they elected a new "pope" who took the name Alexander V. So now there were three men all claiming to be pope, only one of whom actually was. With so many popes at once, it was only a matter of time before one of them figured out how to solve this issue.

This man was the successor of Alexander V, anti-pope John XXIII (not to be confused with Saint John XXIII in the 20th century). In 1414, anti-pope John XXIII called the Council of Constance to try and settle this issue once and for all. He was tired of seeing all of the fighting going on within the Church and knew *if the fighting continued the Church would never accomplish the mission given to her by Jesus.* Pope Gregory XII, who was at this time the legitimate pope in Rome, agreed to the Council, therefore making its decision valid, unlike the Council of Pisa a few years earlier. The idea was for each man to resign his office, therefore letting everyone know the real pope had resigned, and then elect a new pope. Both Gregory XII and John XXIII agreed to resign, but the council had to excommunicate Benedict XIII because he refused. (Pope Benedict XVI became the first pope to resign his office since Pope Gregory XII did it in 1414.) The Cardinals then elected Martin V to be the new pope, ending the nightmare known as the Western Schism.

Now lets be perfectly clear here for at least one second, because this whole mess is, well, a mess. It's confusing, difficult to understand, and incredibly unfortunate. The French Cardinals who left Rome had ABSOLUTELY no authority to declare the election of Pope Urban VI invalid, even if they were pressured. Regardless of how he became pope, he was the pope. And there is no impeachment process for the papacy. Either the pope dies or resigns his office, but it cannot be taken from him. There have been some incredibly terrible popes, *but what they did and how they became pope doesn't make them any less the Successor of St. Peter.*

Thanks be to God, the same can be said of all of us: no matter how much we sin or how much we screw up, we will always be adopted sons and daughters of God. And this is good news because the reality is that there have only been two people who never sinned and they both belong to the Holy Family. For the rest of us, sin is a reality, and if you are like me, it is a daily reality. But despite our sinfulness, God still wants to work through us. Despite our sinfulness, and through His grace, we can still be instruments of God's love in the world.

This is why Jesus sent the Holy Spirit to guide and protect the Church, to lead us "into all Truth" (John 16:13). He knew that, left to our own devices, we would fail. But He also knew that, with His help, we could succeed in changing the world, in spreading His message, and in growing His Church. It is when we cooperate with God's grace that we are able to overcome our sins and be the men and women that God created us to be. So let us pursue that grace even more fervently now. Let us approach our God in prayer, let us receive the sacraments with devotion, and let us always remember that God is greater than our flaws.

REFLECTION QUESTIONS:

1. Do you struggle with pride? Think of three selfless acts you can do this week that will help you be less prideful and commit to doing all three.

2. Do you ever feel frustrated with people in the Church? How does the story of the Western Schism give you hope that the Holy Spirit works in spite of the people in the Church?

3. If you were in a position of authority, would you have resigned your position (like the pope did during the Western Schism) so that the confusion and trouble would end? What would make this hard for you?

10

THE CRUSADES' MISUNDERSTOOD SISTER
– THE INQUISITION –

I love being outdoors, especially when you can get away from the city for a bit and really be in nature. I love to hike and camp, and just encounter God's glory in His creation. Just recently, my wife and I went camping with some friends of ours who have a toddler. Throughout the weekend, their toddler fell down. A lot. It's one of the adorable hazards of being a toddler. I noticed something interesting though: whenever he fell he would look up and as long as we weren't looking directly at him, he wouldn't cry. He would just get himself up and dust himself off. So those few times that he did start crying we knew that he was making it a bigger deal than it needed to be.

People who don't like the Church, or who don't know better, often do the same thing with the Inquisition: they cry and make a bigger deal about it than they need to. Yes, there were some bad things that happened. And, no, that's not okay. But more often than not, stories about the Inquisition are greatly exaggerated.

The Inquisition was started by Pope Innocent III, who was one of the most powerful and influential popes in the history of the Church. And that's because **one of the unintended consequences of the Crusades was most of Europe became allies with the pope,**

and looked to him for some sort of guidance. By the end of the Crusades, all of these different nations had been fighting on the same side for almost 200 years! And they fought in the name of the Church, led by the pope. Pope Innocent III took advantage of this, getting virtually every king, emperor, or dictator to submit to the authority of the pope and of the Church. Why did he do this? Not because he was a power-hungry old man, or even because he thought he knew better then everyone else. In fact, Pope Innocent had very pure motives. You might even call them *innocent*.

Pope Innocent wanted to reform the Church, but he knew that in order to do this he had to be free to lead the Church, with no interference by any secular leaders. And for the most part, Pope Innocent was very successful in getting that freedom. Under his leadership the Church began to oblige Catholics to go to confession and receive Holy Communion at least once a year. He also approved the language of transubstantiation, which we still use today to explain how the bread and wine at Mass actually become the body and blood of Jesus Christ.

But not all of Pope Innocent's accomplishments are appreciated today. Perhaps the most controversial of his reforms was the Inquisition (cue dramatic music). *The Inquisition was a legal procedure that was supposed to eliminate heresy.* Remember, Pope Innocent wanted to reform the Church, and one of those things that needed reforming was heresy. He wanted everyone to experience the joy of the fullness of the truth about Jesus Christ and not to settle for incomplete truths. Jesus said, "I came that they may have life, and have it abundantly" (John 10:10) but we need to have the fullness of Jesus in order to have the fullness of life. Unfortunately, in its mission to give people the fullness of Christ, the Inquisition got out of control at times and today gets a very bad, and often undeserved, reputation. Don't get me wrong, lots of things happened during the Inquisition that were terrible and never should have happened. But this is not true for the vast majority of cases, even though it is often portrayed as such.

Before we talk about how the Inquisition actually worked, we have to mention a few very important things:

1. *We can't judge the people of the 13th century based on what we know today.* The world and the culture was a very different place than it is today. The idea of "religious freedom" didn't really exist yet, and while this is a tragedy, we can't condemn people for not believing in it. At this point in time, if you lived in a Catholic country, you were

expected to believe all the Catholic Church taught. If you didn't, it was thought that your soul was in danger of eternal damnation (which is worse than it sounds) **and** that you were a threat to the unity of society. So heresy was often not just a religious problem, it was a societal problem as well.

2. *The Church has since apologized* for the role that she played in the atrocities that were committed during this time.

3. *The purpose of the Inquisition was conversion*, not to stamp out heresy by murdering those who confessed the wrong. The Church recognized that many of the heresies that were prevalent were a matter of misinformation, not of malice.

4. *When we speak of "The Inquisition" we have to remember that we are not talking about one incident.* There were numerous inquisitions run by different people in different places beginning in 1184 and running through the 16th century.

I'm sure that by now you have heard about the Inquisition in some way shape or form. Maybe it was in your history class, where it is often taught that the "big, bad Catholic Church" tortured and killed hundreds, if not thousands of people... including Red Riding Hood's grannie. Fortunately, this isn't the case. At the same time, though, we have to be careful not to sugar-coat history and try to dismiss the terrible things that did happen. It would be an injustice to pretend there weren't people who abused their power and did irreparable damage to others during this time. But it would also be an injustice to pretend like this was the majority of what happened.

THE INNER WORKINGS

So how did the Inquisition work? First, the Church would send judges, known as "Inquisitors" into areas that were said to have lots of heresy. The judge would come to town and ask anyone who was guilty of heresy to come forward and to confess their sins and receive forgiveness. At the end of this grace period, which could last for several months, the actual Inquisition would begin. At this point, people could accuse others of being heretics. The accused would come before the judge and there would be a trial. If the person was found guilty, they would be punished. Now at this point you might be visualizing the torture that often characterizes conversations on the Inquisition. However, **in the vast majority of cases, the punishment for someone who was found guilty during the Inquisition was incredibly lenient.** The most common punishments for those who repented were helping to build a church, lighting a candle, or going on a pilgrimage. What about those who did not repent? The most common punishment was excommunication and exile, not death.

In fact, the trials of the Inquisition were often much more fair than trials done by the secular authorities in every way, shape, and form. The jails were of a higher quality, the methods used were more humane, and the punishments were far more reasonable. And at the time, this was common knowledge. That is why so many people begged to be tried by Inquisition, or intentionally committed a heresy to get out of a secular jail and be put into an Inquisition jail.

Now, this was not always the case. There were Inquisitors who abused their power. One who is often thrown under the proverbial bus is Tomas de Torquemada, an Inquisitor during the Spanish Inquisition. The Spanish Inquisition is often called the most brutal time of the Church, and Torquemada often portrayed as a brutal man. An honest reading of history, however, reveals that while Torquemada may have been severe, he also made a great effort to be more just. In fact, when the Inquisition passed from the hands of the monarchs into the hands of Torquemada, the quality of jails was improved and the use of torture in trials was limited.

Ultimately, we have to admit at least two truths. First, during the Inquisition, some very bad things did happen. Second, the bad things that happened are almost always blown out of proportion.

So why does the Inquisition get such a bad rap? Well, the prevailing theory right now is that the "Black Legend" of the Inquisition began around the same time as the Protestant reformation. People exaggerated the events of the Inquisition in order to paint the Church as an evil monster and convince others to reject her theology. Like when your little brother made stuff up to get you in trouble with your parents. With the invention of the printing press only a few years before, these ideas spread rapidly and have been difficult to overcome. In recent decades, though, modern scholarship has very much vindicated the Church.

In 1994, St. John Paul II, who we will talk about later in this book, called for an investigation into the Inquisition. He gathered Catholic and non-Catholic historians into a committee with the goal of finding the truth about the Inquisition. For the next ten years, these men and women studied the history freely, and in 2004, a report was released known as the "Report of the International Symposium on the Inquisition." I won't attempt to give you all of the details here, but its findings are fascinating and they really help to put the Inquisition into perspective. This symposium found that:

- Torture was rarely used.
- The numbers of people executed during Inquisitions has been greatly exaggerated.
- Trial by Inquisition was far better than trial by secular court.

Is the Church totally innocent here? No, not completely. There were definitely abuses by certain people and perhaps a lack of oversight, especially at the beginning, when Inquisitors were appointed. For this, St. John Paul II publicly apologized to the entire world. As Catholics, it is so important for us to remember that we aren't perfect. Learning from St. John Paul II, it is important for us to apologize when we have messed up and hurt others. At the same time, we have to remember that our sins do not take away the holiness of the Church. God created the Church, and Jesus died to make the Church holy. No matter how bad we mess up, God protects His Church, so even though every single member of the Church is a sinner, the Church herself will always be holy.

REFLECTION QUESTIONS:

1. Why do you think power corrupts people? How can you exercise power in a merciful and just way?

2. How do you deal with people that disagree with you? Is it easier for you to show mercy and understanding or to get angry and defensive?

3. Why is it important to defend the truth of our Church? How do we do this with compassion and respect?

11

CATHOLIC *IS* CHRISTIAN
– THE PROTESTANT REFORMATION –

Think back to the last time you saw something rolling down a big hill – a rock, a ball, that younger sibling who upset you at the wrong time... When that rolling object first gets started, it moves slow and would be easy to stop if desired. But as it keeps going, it becomes harder and harder to stop. Why? Because it gains momentum. This same principle can be applied to our own lives. When we first get started down a particular path, it is easy to stop and turn around and pick another one. But the farther down the path we go, the harder it gets to choose a different one.

The so-called Protestant Reformation is a really good example of this. And I say "so-called" because people like Martin Luther, John Calvin, and King Henry VIII did not *reform* anything, they started something new, but more on that in a moment. This "reformation" really got its start because of the Avignon Papacy and the corruption in the Church during that time.

As was mentioned earlier, the corruption of the Church during the Avignon Papacy really hurt the Church's reputation, and for good reason. For a long time, those who were supposed to be showing us how to love and live like Jesus were more caught up with their own power and wealth than they should have been. Jesus may very well have said to them, like the Pharisees, "This people honors me with their lips, but their heart is far from me" (Matthew 15:8). As respect for the Church diminished, so did trust in the Church's teachings. And these seeds of doubt that were sown were watered and slowly grew until Martin Luther came and reaped them. These seeds were watered by men like John Wycliffe, who rejected the doctrine of transubstantiation and the authority of the pope. They grew under the care of men like Jan Huss, who taught that all people were, from their creation, predestined to go to heaven or hell and who taught that the Bible alone is the ultimate religious authority.

What was sown and watered during the 14th and 15th centuries finally came to fruition in the 16th century. Although he never intended to start a revolution, Martin Luther did just that. In 1517, Martin Luther famously nailed his 95 Theses to the door of the Cathedral in Wittenberg. Often misunderstood, *this was not an act of defiance, but rather an invitation to debate*. Prior to being excommunicated in 1521 Martin Luther was a devout Catholic monk, a member of the Augustinian Order, and someone who had some doubts and questions about certain practices and beliefs of the Church.

A FEW LEGITIMATE COMPLAINTS

Although they hurt the Church, the "reformers" weren't completely wrong. Martin Luther, and many others (including Wycliffe and Hus), pointed out some serious problems going on in the Church. They pointed to things like simony (the buying of a Church position), nepotism (giving positions of authority to family members), poorly educated clergy, political and financial corruption, and the sale of indulgences as practices of the Church that should be stopped. Of all of the things they pointed out as wrong, the sale and abuse of indulgences was the worst.

An indulgence is a grace that removes some of our time in purgatory, making us perfect sooner so that we can get to heaven more quickly. Jesus gave the Church this power when He said to the Apostles "All authority in heaven and on earth has been given to me. Go therefore and make disciples of all nations..." (Matthew 28:18-19) and again "Truly, I say to you, whatever you bind on earth will be bound in heaven, and whatever you loose on earth will be loosed in heaven" (Matthew 18:18).

Now obviously an indulgence is something that people would want. Throughout history, the Church would grant these indulgences for special reasons. For instance, the Church granted indulgences to those who went on the Crusades. Unfortunately, some people in the Church began to abuse indulgences. Certain Church officials started selling indulgences claiming that, "once the coin in the coffer rings, the soul from purgatory springs." This isn't a "Get out of Jail Free" card, though. *Contrary to a very common misconception, receiving an indulgence cannot be substituted for going to confession.*

The selling of indulgences was problematic for at least two reasons. The first reason is that an indulgence is a grace, and **grace is always a free gift.** *It cannot be bought or earned.* God gives us grace freely. Second, grace does not work like magic. We don't just say a few words and "poof" all of our sins go away. No, God wants to actually help us change, to actually become more loving, generous, faithful people, and His grace helps us to do that. But grace only "works" to the extent that we are willing to work with it. The Church uses the word "disposition" to describe our willingness to cooperate with God's grace in becoming better people. Is someone who is buying an indulgence properly "disposed" to remove sin from their lives? Probably not. It should also be noted that this is true of the grace we receive in the sacraments too. That grace won't work like magic, we have to be willing to work with it, and work hard, to make sure to make it a reality. Just because I received the Sacrament of Matrimony doesn't mean I am automatically the perfect husband (just ask my wife). But with God's grace I can become a better husband each and every day.

COMPLAINTS TURNED TO REJECTION

Many of the complaints of the "reformers" were legitimate. They highlighted some very serious errors in the practice of the Church; there were plenty of things happening that should not have been happening. And Martin Luther got it right when he said that things needed to change. Unfortunately though, after Luther posted his 95 Theses for debate, momentum took charge and Luther quickly found himself rejecting key teachings of the Church, like the authority of the pope, and then removing books from the Bible that opposed his new theology. Luther was officially excommunicated from the Church on January 3, 1521 because his teachings could no longer be reconciled with the faith that Jesus gave to His Apostles.

But Luther started something that was bigger. His rejection of Church authority inspired others to also reject that authority. People like John Calvin and King Henry VIII followed in Luther's footsteps, declaring that the Church had no authority. For some, this rejection of Church authority came on theological grounds. For others, it was a political decision. Either way, the Church recognized that people were leaving behind the life-giving teachings of Jesus Christ and were replacing them with teachings that were easier and more comfortable. In response to all of these challenges, the Church called a council to clarify the teachings that had been given to her by Jesus. And so, in the year 1545, the Council of Trent began.

The Council of Trent was undoubtedly one of the most important events in the history of the Church. Until this time, the Church had not formally declared certain teachings, mostly because they had never been challenged. It was at the Council of Trent that the Church *formally* declared which books belong in the Bible. This isn't because they had been changing throughout history. In fact, the books that were declared to be a part of Scripture had been used almost universally since the Synod of Rome in the year 382 AD.

Here is a list of the major reforms that were instituted at the Council of Trent in response to the "reformers:"

- Officially declared the Canon of Scripture.
- Officially declared the seven sacraments.
- Established a seminary system to better educate men for the priesthood.
- Called bishops to a life of greater poverty and made them be present in their diocese.
- Reaffirmed the celibate life for priests.
- Outlawed simony (buying and selling positions of authority in the Church), nepotism (giving positions of power to friends or family, despite their qualifications), and the selling the selling of indulgences.

There were many other reforms, but these were the most prevalent because they answered the challenges of the reformers.

A PRAYER FOR RE-UNIFICATION

Ever since the Protestant Reformation, there has been disunity among followers of Jesus Christ. Those who left the Catholic Church abandoned the ship of salvation which God gave to the world. *But they are not lost.* The Church, together with these Christian denominations, works toward re-unification. Through the process known as *ecumenism,* the Church is striving to regain the unity that has been lost, the unity that Jesus wanted for his people (John 17:21). There have been great strides towards the reunification of Christians, but this process can only continue if we are willing to work and pray for it. When I was still new to my faith I used to view non-Catholic Christians as my enemy. I thought that they were blind and ignorant and lacked faith. But as I have grown and matured, I have realized that the exact opposite is true: they are not our enemies but our separated brothers and sisters, adopted sons and daughters of God, just like we are. God loves them just as much as He loves us. There are many faithful Lutherans and Baptists I know who are more faithful to the teachings of Jesus than some Catholics I know. God wants us to learn from one another and to restore the unity that He gave to us.

So, what role can you play in bringing about the unity that Jesus prayed for?

First, *Pray for it!* Prayer is absolutely the most important thing that any of us can do. Prayer will soften our hearts and allow us to get past the personal biases we may have and love one another the way we ought to.

Second, *Read good Catholic books* and know your faith well. Know your faith well enough to be able to explain what you believe and why you believe it.

Third, *Don't be afraid to talk about your faith.* If people don't know that Jesus is a big part of your life then they will never talk to you about Him. And if they don't ever talk to you about Him then it will be difficult to help them love Him.

Fourth, and this is so important, when you talk to non-Catholic Christians, *do not approach them with an "I am right you are wrong, you need to convert now" mindset.* No matter what we do, we cannot force people to accept the authentic teachings of Christ. All we can do is explain what we believe and why we believe it and then ask the Holy Spirit to do His work.

Fifth, and most importantly, *love those who disagree with you.* No matter how well you know Church teaching and no matter how good you are at explaining it, people will still disagree with you. It's okay. It doesn't make them a bad person or even a bad Christian. It just means that they are at a different place in their journey with Jesus right now. Just because you disagree with someone doesn't mean you should stop loving them. It may be difficult, but if we don't love them we are not upholding the teachings of Jesus.

The Protestant Reformation is certainly a sad time in Church history because we as humans did so much damage to the Church. But

Jesus promised us that the Church would last forever, and He is true to His word. By the grace of the Holy Spirit, the Catholic Church emerged from the Reformation wounded, but soon recovered and gained new life through the teachings of the Council of Trent. Armed with those teachings, the Church went back into the world and brought more people to Jesus Christ.

REFLECTION QUESTIONS:

1. When have you experienced God's grace? How does this experience support the Church's teaching that grace is freely given to us?

2. There are five ways we can bring about unity (prayer, read good Catholic books, talk about our faith, don't approach with a "convert now" mentality, and love those who disagree with you) – which is hardest for you? Which is easiest?

3. Challenge: Talk about faith with a non-Catholic friend.

12

THE GIFT OF FAITH *AND* REASON
– THE ENLIGHTENMENT –

If you ask people who know me, they will probably tell you that I have an ego. I tend to be bad at being humble. This is mostly true. I'm working on it, but I am still not great at it. There have been moments in my life, though, that have really humbled me, that have made me realize that I am small and that only God is big. I remember the day that I asked my wife to marry me and how humbled I was when she said yes. I knew that on my own I could never love her the way she deserves to be loved, that without God I would never be enough. I remember my first day as a teacher, looking at all of my students and being terrified that I would never be able to help them love God, or worse, that I would lead them away from Him and only have a millstone to look forward to (if you don't get the joke, go read Mark 9:42).

In moments like these, God reminds me of the young boy from the story of the feeding of the 5,000 in the Gospel of John (John 6:1-14). This boy brought five loaves of bread and two fish to Jesus, and Jesus made it enough for the people. Our God is a God of creating something out of nothing. He has done it so many times in my own life and I'm sure that if you think really hard you can remember at least one time when He did it in yours.

But our God loves us so much that He doesn't just want to make something out of nothing, He wants to turn the evils in our lives into something good. And our God is the master at turning something bad into something good, just look at the Crucifixion.

This is what God has done with the Protestant Reformation. The break in the unity of the Church is not what God wants. We can recognize it as bad, and yet God used even this tragedy to bring about something good in the Church: the Council of Trent and the Counter Reformation. **The Counter Reformation renewed the Church and helped to more clearly identify her as God's one, holy, catholic, and apostolic Church.**

But just because God brought something good out of the Protestant Reformation doesn't mean that there weren't negative consequences. Unfortunately, the divisions amongst the followers of Christ caused great strife. In fact, for the next 100 years, Europe experienced a series of wars in which religion played a role. The last of these "religious wars" was the 30 years war, ending in 1648 with the Treaty of Westphalia. It was out of this climate that the Enlightenment ideas began to grow. As people grew more and more fed up with religion, they began to look for answers elsewhere. The Enlightenment, which historians say lasted from around the 1650's until the end of the 18th century, was good for the world in one major way: *People began to use reason to explore the world.*

THE IMPORTANCE OF REASON

The use of reason is so important. It allows us to analyze a situation and to come to good conclusions. It was during the enlightenment that science and technology really began to grow into what they are today. The problem with the enlightenment was the same as its major benefit: the use of human reason. *Because of original sin, our minds are, in a sense, darkened. We have difficulty knowing the truth perfectly. We are tempted to act selfishly and to only accept what we want to be true.* We do this all the time, we justify things to ourselves so that we don't feel so bad doing them. It might be telling yourself that homework isn't that important so its not a big deal if you copy your friends assignment since you didn't do yours – sorry that's the teacher in me. Or maybe it's telling yourself that the lie you just told was for a good cause. Whatever the case may be, the point is that our human reason is often flawed. The emphasis on reason during the Enlightenment was good, but *the major error of the Enlightenment was claiming that human reason alone was enough.*

This emphasis on human reason began to crowd out the importance of religion. It came to be that religious beliefs were seen as superstitions instead of valid ideas and people who held those beliefs were seen at best as naïve, and at worst, a threat to society. Christianity was expected to be a matter of private expression and therefore began to have less and less influence in politics, culture, and even education, a trend which we are seeing again today. These Enlightenment ideas came to their climax in the French Revolution at the end of the 18th century.

The French Revolution is a great example of the influence of the Enlightenment. During the French Revolution, the Church in France was almost destroyed. French priests were forced to take oaths of loyalty to France instead of to the Church, France was de-Christianized to the point that statues of the "goddess of reason" were set up in Catholic Churches and they were re-named "Temples of Reason." France, the Church's Eldest Daughter, a country that had been Catholic for over a thousand years, had suddenly fallen into atheism.

The **French Revolution** is indeed an example of how weak human reason is and how much we do need God. During the French Revolution between 30,000 and 50,000 people across France were executed. But, at the end of it all, the faith of the people of France triumphed and in 1801 the Catholic Church was reinstated in France to the joy of many people.

LOST FAITH

The extensive arm of the Enlightenment didn't end there. With all of the emphasis on human reason and the mockery of religious belief, the Church found herself unable to make a positive difference in the lives of many people. The Church was an outcast, the person at your school that nobody wants to talk to. They just didn't trust the Church. If people don't trust the Church, then they are missing out on an invaluable source of God's power in their lives. If we don't look to the Church when we try to hear God's voice, where can we look?

The popes in the 19th century realized this and tried to steer people back to faith in God and trust in the Church. It was Pope Pius IX who perhaps did the most to help bring people back to faith in the Church. Pope Pius IX issued what he called a "Syllabus of Errors" in 1864. In this document Pope Pius IX pointed out many of the errors that society was making at the time. His goal was not to point fingers or place blame, but to help people realize that there were mistakes that were hurting society and those errors needed to be fixed. This document, as you might guess, was not the most popular. We as people tend to not like being told that we are messing up. But Pius pointed out a truth that people needed to hear, and that we too need to hear: *Not every opinion is equally valid.*

There are a lot of opinions out there on what we should do and how we should do it: some are good and some are bad, some are closer to the truth and some are further from it. Pope Pius IX reminded us, that because of original sin, we sometimes have a hard time differentiating between good and bad, right and wrong. Especially if the wrong choice seems like "fun." He reminded the world that we need to consult our Creator, and we encounter Him most perfectly in the Church.

THE FIRST VATICAN COUNCIL

But one document was not going to get his point across; Pope Pius needed more. To get this extra push, he called the First Vatican Council in 1869. It was at this council that the Church clarified that *faith and reason are always in agreement with one another since God is the author of both.* The Church, however, placed a greater emphasis on faith, because God cannot make an error but humans can. Second, and some might say more importantly, the Church clarified her teaching on the infallibility of the pope. Now this doesn't mean that everything the pope says is perfectly true. It means that, in certain situations, the Holy Spirit gives to the pope the gift of speaking without error. What are those conditions? Good question.

- The pope must be speaking *ex cathedra* or "from the chair" of St. Peter. This doesn't mean that he is literally sitting in the chair, but that he is intentionally acting as the shepherd of the whole Church.

- The pope must be making a formal teaching on matters of faith and/or morals. That means he must intend that whatever he is saying must be believed and/or lived out.

This isn't a teaching that the Church just made up one day. In fact, the Church has always looked to St. Peter and his successors to lead and guide the Church. Plus, it wouldn't really make sense if the pope did not have this authority. Let's think about this for one moment. Does it make sense to you that God, the King of Kings and Lord of

Lords would create a Church that He intends to use to bring the whole world to salvation, would die on a cross for that Church, and then leave the Church in the hands of fallen, sinful humans who can barely make good fashion choices, let alone theological ones? I think not. Although Jesus made Peter the head of the Church, He also sent the Church the Holy Spirit to make sure that we wouldn't mess up the message like a giant game of "telephone" (John 16:13). Jesus tells Peter that the Church will live forever (Matthew 16:18) not because Peter and his successors are special on their own, but because the Holy Spirit will be present and, by His blessing, will make their work enough.

This is the great gift of God, that when we give Him everything, when we trust Him completely, even though it can never be enough, He transforms it into enough by His grace. So I urge you, trust in God completely. Give Him all of your efforts, your love, and your strength, because you never know what He can do with just five loaves and two fishes.

REFLECTION QUESTIONS:

1. Do you feel like there is a tension between faith and reason? Where do you feel like there is the most tension?

2. Why isn't human reason enough for us to understand the world we live in? How would you explain the important role of faith and reason to someone?

3. What is one teaching of the Church that you struggle with understanding? How can you learn more about this teaching over the next few weeks?

13

A DIVINE SOFTWARE UPDATE
– VATICAN II –

You may not remember what life was like before smart phones existed... let me fill you in a little bit. Smart phones definitely have their benefits. We, back in the olden days, used to make CDs so that we would have music with us in the car, or wait until we got home to post about our lives on Facebook. If we wanted to take pictures or videos on vacation we needed to carry an extra device. Heck, we used to have to look up addresses and print off directions before we left the house! But there was at least one major benefit to life without smartphones: arguments weren't ever won or lost. If you disagreed with me on something, you couldn't just take out your phone and prove me wrong. And I don't like to hear that I am wrong because being wrong means I have to change, and change is hard. But there are plenty of times when change is necessary.

The Catholic Church encountered one of these moments in the middle of the 20th century. In the year 1962 St. John XXIII called the 2nd Vatican Council, which caused some very dramatic changes in the Church. These changes however, were not changes in belief, but changes in practice. St. John XXIII recognized that the Church needed to re-examine her relationship with the world. The world had changed so much, even since the first Vatican Council about 100 years earlier. The pope wanted to see change because he wanted the world to be able to better understand the Church and therefore be more able to accept the Church and her message of love and salvation.

The Church needed a software update. Everything worked fine, but the pope believed there was a better way to do things. The way that the Church lived and prayed was not the way that many people encountered God. So St. John XXIII called Vatican II with the goal of "*aggiornamento*," or of updating and renewing the words and actions of the Church. If you think of the Church as a building, you could say that he wanted to open the doors and the windows and let the fresh air in! He wanted to translate Jesus' message into the modern language of the world so that Jesus could be heard and accepted by all.

The Second Vatican Council was historic in many ways. It was the first Church council in which members of other faiths were able to participate through discussion; it was the first council in which the media played a large role; it was the largest gathering of bishops from around the world; and it was the only council called not to address a specific issue, but rather simply to discuss the practices of the Church and how they could be improved. The bishops present had a very serious task at hand: How can we help others better know, love, and accept Jesus Christ and His Church? Their answer was brilliant.

The bishops chose to make some very important reforms that helped to refresh and renew the Church while maintaining the teachings and beliefs that Jesus gave to the Apostles and have been handed down ever since. Here is a very brief list of some of the more prominent and impactful results of the Council.

RENEWED EFFORTS OF ECUMENISM
Ecumenism is the movement to restore the unity of Jesus' Church. Since the Second Vatican Council, the Church has made more and more efforts to reach out to our Protestant brothers and sisters and to work through our differences. Today, we pray together and talk more often than before, and these renewed efforts have brought many Christians back to Jesus' one Church.

RENEWED CALL TO HOLINESS
Believe it or not, there was a time when people believed that only bishops, priests, and members of religious orders were called to be holy. Vatican II made it clear that we as Catholics, and in fact all

Christians, have the responsibility to lead holy lives. This is called the universal call to holiness. Mother Teresa said it best: "Holiness is not the luxury of the few, but the simple duty of you and I." We don't have to achieve perfection here on Earth, but we need to do our best to follow in the footsteps of Jesus and to love as He did.

THE ROLE OF THE LAITY

The laity is a Church term, which simply means those members of the Church who aren't ordained or consecrated. So, anyone who isn't a deacon, priest, or bishop, or a religious brother or sister (monk/nun) is a member of the laity. Prior to Vatican II, the laity (you and I) did not play a large role in the Mass. But because the bishops renewed the universal call to holiness, they also believed it was important to allow the laity to participate more and more in the Mass. Thanks to Vatican II, lay members of the Church can be lectors, extraordinary ministers of holy communion, sacristans, etc.

THE USE OF THE VERNACULAR LANGUAGE IN THE LITURGY

Speaking of the Mass, did you ever notice that you can understand the Mass? That is thanks to Vatican II. Prior to the Council, the liturgy was celebrated in Latin all over the world. This helped to maintain the universality of the Church. The Council, however, recognized that people had difficulty understanding and participating in the Mass because it was in Latin. Therefore, the bishops said that it was fitting for the liturgy to be celebrated in the common language of the people, which we call the "vernacular language." This allows us to participate more freely in the liturgy and to truly see the beauty of the prayers of the Church.

These were just some of the major changes that we see in the Church, but there were also many other things that happened at the council. In fact, the Second Vatican Council published 16 different documents covering topics like the role of the bishops, divine revelation, the importance of religious freedom, and the Church's relationship with other religions.

The Second Vatican Council, however, was not all sunshine and rainbows. Although the ideas of the council were good, problems quickly arose when the Church began to put those ideas into practice. I know this feeling all too well. A couple of years ago I started a new hobby: woodworking. I bought some tools and some wood, then downloaded the blueprints to the world's most simple table, and got to work. With clear instructions and new tools, the project should have been easy. Four days later I never wanted to cut another piece of wood again. I finished the project and suddenly wished I had never started. My table was crooked, lopsided, uneven, and just plain ugly. Now it hides behind the couch in my house and when people ask about it I quickly change the subject.

Something similar happened after Vatican II. Although the Council had given the Church a blueprint showing what the end result should be, the process to get there was a little bumpy. Thankfully, the Holy Spirit is far more concerned with the way the Church functions than how pretty my table is (although, a little help with my table would have been nice).

The problems that developed out of the Second Vatican Council developed because people either misunderstood or wrongly applied the teachings of the council, just like my misunderstanding of the directions for my table. It wasn't that the council was wrong or that their ideas were bad, but that *we as fallen humanity find it difficult to carry out God's plan perfectly.* Perhaps the biggest difficulties that arose came from people's misunderstanding of the purpose of the council. The purpose of the council was, according to St. John Paul II, (who participated in the council), to "guard and present better the precious deposit of Christian doctrine in order to make it more accessible to the Christian faithful and to all people of good will." In other words, to find new ways to make the Gospel message attractive to people living in modern society, a society which was very different from the one in which the Church began.

Unfortunately, some bishops misunderstood this to mean that they should slacken the moral restrictions of God Himself, so that people would not be hurt when they were told that something was wrong. Other members of the Church also lowered their moral standards because they thought that incorporating the values of the world into the Church would make the Church more attractive to the world. This type of "reaching out" seems like it works for a while: If the Church adopts the practices of the world, then yes, more people might join the Church, and she would definitely be more popular. And if the Church's purpose was to be popular then that would be the right way to go. But that's not the Church's purpose. **The Church exists to bring God's salvation to the world, and she can only do this if she remains faithful to what God taught.**

The problem with the Church conforming to the world is that it's the opposite of what is supposed to happen. We need to conform ourselves to God, not try to make God more like us. Jesus told His Apostles that remaining faithful to His teachings would be wildly unpopular. Jesus says to them, "Blessed are you when men revile you and persecute you and utter all kinds of evil against you falsely on my account" (Matthew 5: 11) and, "If the world hates you, know that it has hated me before it hated you"(John 15:18). This is why, despite the errors that some members of the Church made, and despite pressure from all sides to change her teachings regarding certain things, the Church will always remain faithful to the teachings of Jesus, no matter how few people choose to accept them.

Despite all of these difficulties, many people *really* understood Vatican II and put its teachings into practice well. They were people who brought the Church into the new era, who helped to further the Gospel message, and who have almost definitely impacted your life, whether you know it or not. But one person stands out particularly from this crowd. One man who was present at the council and who really embodied everything that the council stood for. His name was Karol Wojtyla.

REFLECTION QUESTIONS:

1. The Second Vatican Council renewed the call for all people to be holy. How do you strive for holiness in your life?

2. Vatican II called for greater participation of the laity in liturgy. Are you involved in liturgical ministry at your parish? If so, what do you enjoy most about it? If not, how can you become more involved?

3. Why is ecumenism important? How can you work toward this effort in your life?

14

NEW HERALDS OF FAITH
– ST. JOHN PAUL II AND THE MODERN CHURCH –

A couple of years ago I was teaching an 8th grade Confirmation class in Wisconsin. One day when we didn't have class, we just got together and had fun. So, as a class, we went to the school gym to play basketball, and I remember one girl defied me to make a three-point shot. No, not defy, she taunted me saying I couldn't do it. She passed me a ball and I took the shot. I want to be **very** clear here: I am **not** a good basketball player. In fact, some people might describe me as a terrible basketball player. I'm the opposite of LeBron James: I'm bad at basketball and I don't whine very much. But on this day, for some reason, the ball went through the hoop, and I played it cool as if that always happened. The girl looked stunned and said, "No way you can do that again!" So I got the ball back, and by some miracle of the Holy Spirit I made my second basket in a row. And this girl just stared at me as if everything she was ever taught had just been proven wrong, like her whole universe was falling apart. She opened her mouth and said, "But that's impossible. You're Catholic, you can't be good at sports!"

We often have this misconception of people we view as holy: we think they aren't "normal" people just like us. I fall into this trap all the time. I always forget to invite my priest friends to come with me whenever we are going bowling, or paintballing, or doing something fun. I think we make this mistake with the pope a lot too. We look at the pope and see his funny hat and robes and forget that he is just like the rest of us, a person fighting sin and struggling to be like Christ, a sinner in need of a Savior. But there have been a few popes in recent years who have really shown us the human side of the papacy.

Most recently, Pope Francis has helped changed the perception of the papacy for many people. Since he was elected in March of 2013, Pope Francis has been a beacon of hope for Catholics and non-Catholics all over the world. He has shown the world God's love and compassion in a way that some thought was impossible for the "big, bad Catholic Church." But even before Pope Francis, there was another pope who drastically changed how people thought of the papacy and how they viewed the Catholic Church: **St. John Paul II**.

St. John Paul II was not your typical pope, and he seemed to really "break the mold" of what people expected of him. First of all, he was an athlete. And I do mean an athlete. Prior to becoming pope, St. John Paul II, who was born Karol Wojtyla (pronounced Voy-tee-wuh), was an avid hiker, skier, camper, fisherman, and soccer player. Even during his days as a priest and a teacher, he would take students on camping trips to experience the beauty of the world and to encounter the God who had created that beauty. He was incredibly intelligent, and wonderfully humble, but he came from a very difficult background.

As a young boy, Karol experienced a lot of suffering. His mother died when he was just nine years old, and his older brother, who was a doctor, died only three years later. His father was a member of the army and they lived a very simple life. As he grew older, Karol took on many odd jobs, even working in a mining quarry to help provide for his father. As a young boy, Karol always showed promise in his studies, but he went far beyond anything that anyone had ever expected from him.

In 1938, at the age of 18, Karol enrolled at the University in Krakow in Poland. He loved to write and to act and he had dreams of pursuing writing and acting in his life. But just one year later, in 1939, Poland was invaded by Nazi forces who closed the University and set out to destroy the Polish culture. Many of Karol's friends resisted the Nazis by fighting against them, but Karol believed that there was another way to resist them. He and his friends began an underground theatre to preserve Polish culture. To some this may seem a little silly. How could you fight the Nazis through theatre? Well, the Nazis wanted to eliminate what made the Polish people Polish. That's why they closed the universities, so that people could not educate themselves. They set out to destroy the rich literature of the Polish people, hoping to leave Poland with no legacy whatsoever. Karol knew that the Nazi occupation could not last forever, but that if they succeeded in destroying the Polish culture then Poland might disappear. He set about to preserve the culture so that when the Nazis were gone, Poland would remain. He and some of his friends would memorize poetry, novels, put on plays, etc. so that the Polish culture would remain alive and well.

His heroics were not over yet, nor would this be the last time that Karol did anything in secret. Beginning in 1942, Karol answered God's call to the priesthood and enrolled in the seminary in Krakow. The Nazis though had shut down the seminaries, so Karol entered a secret seminary in the bishop's house. When he was ordained a priest, he taught at the recently re-opened University in Krakow, and began to write. He did such good work as a priest that he was eventually made the Archbishop of Krakow. As a priest and a bishop, Karol worked hard to resist the Communist regime that had taken over when the Nazis left Poland. He demanded that people's rights be respected and that the Church be allowed to worship. He organized demonstrations, prayed with protesters, said Mass publicly, even while the Communist government tried to find a way to lessen his influence. Finally, on October 16, 1978, Karol Wojtyla was elected pope and took the name John Paul II, remembering his predecessor Pope John Paul I, who died after only 33 days as pope.

As pope, he radically changed how people viewed the papacy and the Catholic Church. Pope John Paul I's predecessor, Pope Paul VI, made many people view the papacy and the Church in a negative light. Not because he was a bad guy or a bad pope, but because of his encyclical "**Humanae Vitae**." Today, "Humanae Vitae" is famous for declaring that all forms of artificial birth control are contrary to the dignity of the person and therefore must not be used. He said that if artificial birth control became widespread we would at least four things happen: First, a general lowering of moral standards; second, a rise in infidelity among married couples; third, men would come to respect women less; and fourth, governments would force reproductive technologies on their citizens. This declaration was incredibly unpopular. Many people felt that the Church was "out of touch with reality" and they rejected Pope Paul VI and his teachings. They saw him as an "old man" who was living in another time. Unfortunately, since 1968, all of his predictions have come true. Despite the anger that stirred up against the Church during Pope Paul VI's papacy, St John Paul II managed to help people love the Church again.

It began with his personality. St. John Paul II was incredibly likeable. He was like your favorite grandpa who always had candy in his pockets. He was also unbelievably humble and radiated the love of God to all people. St. John Paul II was the most travelled pope in history, visiting more than half of all the countries in the world. He was highly visible to people, prayed constantly, and loved God with his whole heart. Even if he had not been a priest, it would have been obvious to anyone who met him that he had fallen in love with Jesus Christ. He did more than just show people what it looked like to love Jesus and His Church though; he helped bring people back to the Church.

In 1986, St. John Paul II held the first ever **World Youth Day.** He instituted this event as a way for young people from all over the world to come together and to pray in solidarity with one another and to share and grow in their faith. That same year, he called for a catechism to be written. After years of writing and revision, the Catechism of the Catholic Church was approved by St. John Paul II and published it so that the world could better know what the Church teaches and why she teaches it. In 2002, St. John Paul II added the **Luminous Mysteries**, or the Mysteries of Light, to the Rosary. These mysteries focus our attention on Jesus' public life and works, and combined with the Joyful, Sorrowful, and Glorious Mysteries, give us a more complete picture of who Jesus is when we meditate on the rosary. But, the most influential aspects of his legacy are not the Luminous Mysteries, or the Catechism of the Catholic Church, or even World Youth Day. The two most impactful teachings of St. John Paul II's papacy are his theology of the body and his call for a new evangelization.

Beginning in 1979, St. John Paul II gave a series of 129 public teachings that were later called his **"Theology of the Body."** In these audiences, St. John Paul II sought to help us understand what our body tells us about who we are as adopted sons and daughters of God. Remember that unpopular letter from Pope Paul VI called Humanae Vitae? St. John Paul II gave these audiences as a means of explaining the theology behind this letter. His starting point was simple: Since we are created by God in God's own image and likeness (Genesis 1:27), then our bodies must tell us something about who God is and what He intended for us. As the pope developed this idea, it continued to grow and grow, so much so that it took him five years to present the basic outline of it to the Church during his weekly public speaking addresses. He would continue to expand these ideas in his later homilies, Audiences, and writings. His teachings in the Theology of the Body range everywhere from how the human person can only find true happiness when he makes himself a gift to others, to the proper role of sex and sexuality within our life, to understanding and living out the Sacrament of Marriage, but it is all rooted in the incredible dignity that you and I have as sons and daughters of the King.

St. John Paul II's other most impactful contribution came in 1990 when his encyclical *Redemptoris Missio* was published. In this encyclical, St. John Paul II discussed how the Church evangelizes and wrote about the need for a new evangelization. This call became a rallying cry for people all over the world, and it continues today. **The New Evangelization** is not a new teaching of the Church, nor is it a flashy video or popular music, but *a renewed effort to help people fall in love with the person of Jesus Christ.* The New Evangelization is a lot like the Second Vatican Council in that it calls us to find new ways to preach same Gospel message. But it doesn't only call us to find new ways, it calls us to a new effort. Think about it, when was the last time you evangelized? Do you even know what evangelization is? St. John Paul II said that this new evangelization is the duty of everyone, and that "No believer in Christ, no Christian institution can avoid this supreme duty: to proclaim Christ to all peoples."

The job of evangelization is not just my job, or your youth minister's job, or your pastor's job, it is your job too! You can evangelize in the way you treat others, especially those who hurt you. You can evangelize by doing your schoolwork well and doing it right. You can evangelize by saying grace before meals, even when your friends look at you weird. You can evangelize by inviting your friends to pray with you and to come to Mass with you. And when you do these little things with great love and respect for others, people will ask why you do them, and that is your opportunity to tell them about the person of Jesus. But we must renew our efforts. Too often we leave the "Church stuff" to others and we don't bring Jesus with us everywhere we go. Without you and I, the new evangelization cannot succeed. Without "u," the "Church" is not complete.

A person who has done a great job of living out the New Evangelization is Pope Francis. His election was historic in that he was the first pope from the Jesuit order, the first pope from Latin America, and the first non-European pope in more than 1,200 years. Pope Francis has done a marvelous job of getting people to look at the Church in a new light, even though he is often misquoted, misunderstood, and people feel like he will change Church teaching for the first time ever (spoiler alert: he won't). Pope Francis has encouraged us to focus more on loving people first, rather than leading with doctrine. Notice I didn't write, "forget doctrine", or "anything goes." The doctrine of the Church is still important, but before we teach people the doctrine of the Church, we must introduce them to the person of Jesus Christ, to the person who loves them unconditionally and will always be there to help them.

This is the heart of the new evangelization, putting people back into relationship with Jesus Christ. And once they love Jesus and want to follow Him, then we can start talking about how we properly follow Jesus and what He asks of us. As Father Raniero Cantalamessa, preacher to the Papal Household, once put it, *"Christianity does not begin by telling us what we must do. Christianity begins by telling us what God has done for us through Jesus Christ."*

And this isn't just the heart of the new evangelization, it's also the heart of the Gospel message. Jesus Christ came to put is back into right relationship with God, so that we could have life to the fullest. He came to give us the gift of a new life, and now it's our turn to share that gift with the world.

REFLECTION QUESTIONS:

1. *"Christianity does not begin by telling us what we must do. Christianity begins by telling us what God has done for us through Jesus Christ."* How can we joyfully share our faith with others?

2. Take a few minutes to write down your conversion story. How did you come to know Jesus Christ?

3. What creative and innovative ways can you use to share your faith with others? How can you be a part of the "new evangelization?"

– EPILOGUE –
THE UNIVERSAL CALL TO SAINTHOOD
– THE FUTURE IS YOURS –

Even though this book is over, the story most certainly is not; the Kingdom is still journeying toward ultimate fulfillment. Those who came before us have done a great job and they have built a beautiful, solid foundation. It started with Peter, the rock on whom Jesus built the Church (Matthew 16:18), and the Apostles, who preached the message of Jesus Christ and gave their lives so that others might know Him. Through their preaching and their courage, they inspired a new generation of believers who refused to give up on their faith no matter what the cost. These martyrs suffered bravely at the hands of the Roman Empire, finally receiving the legal right to their faith after centuries of pain. It is abundantly clear how the martyrs helped to build the Kingdom, and yet still the Kingdom was incomplete.

As Christianity became more widespread, something was needed to replace the blood of the martyrs in helping the Church grow, and many great theologians were ready to answer the call. Men like Athanasius and Cyril of Alexander helped to build God's Kingdom on earth by protecting the truth that was being attacked. By combatting heresy and preserving God's Word, countless saints helped the Church to grow, but there was still work to be done.

The Crusaders (tried to) literally build the Kingdom by reconquering the land in which the Church had begun. They set out to make the

Holy Land a safe place for pilgrims again, and even though they didn't succeed, they still played an important part in God's Kingdom.

And in every difficulty that the Church faced, there were always great saints ready to do the hard work that it took to build up the Kingdom. We talked about numerous ones in this book, like St. Polycarp, St. Ignatius, St. Catherine of Sienna, St. John XXIII, St. John Paul II, and others. But there were also many who we did not talk about, like St. Faustina, St. Maximillian Kolbe, St. Edith Stein, and so many more, all with unique stories and contributions to God's Kingdom here on earth. But before they were great saints, they were ordinary people, struggling to overcome their sins and to live faithfully according to the Gospel. This is what makes them so incredible: That they were just like you and I and yet they are radical examples of love and faith!

Within each one of us there is a great saint. All we must do is to continue to say, "yes," to God and, "no," to sin. It sounds easy, but as I am sure you know by now, it is not always so simple. But we must make the effort, we must strive for sainthood, because if we don't, we will miss our part of the story God wants to tell through us. That is how much God trusts you. He has given you a task that only you can accomplish. He has made you a unique individual and has asked you to help build the Kingdom in a way that only you can.

Yes, within that call lies a lot of responsibility, but God doesn't expect you to do it alone. In fact, He knows that you cannot do it on your own. That's why God became man, and that's why Jesus sent us the Holy Spirit when He ascended into heaven. God has given us everything we need to accomplish our mission, He has given us every tool to build His Kingdom here on earth, and He is always present to help us when things get difficult.

In the entire history of the Church, there has never been a single obstacle that God could not overcome. At the very beginning of the Church, God overcame the single greatest obstacle there is – death! So no matter what obstacles you are facing in your life right now, I guarantee that God can help you overcome them. So take courage, have faith, and ask the Lord to help you fight the good fight!

Who knows, maybe in another 1,000 years someone will write a book about how you helped to build the Kingdom of God.